Here be Dragons

Youth Work and Mission Off the Map

Richard Passmore
Lorimer Passmore
James Ballantyne

FRONTIER
YOUTH TRUST

© 2013 Richard Passmore, Lorimer Passmore, James Ballantyne

ISBN: 978-0-9927570-0-7

First Published 2013 by Porthouse
for Frontier Youth Trust

Frontier Youth Trust
(S15b) St. Georges Community Hub
Great Hampton Row
Newtown
Birmingham
B19 3JG

www.fyt.org.uk

The views expressed in this book are those of the authors and do not necessarily reflect the views of the publisher.

Cover design by Sam (SPAD) spaduk@hotmail.co.uk

This work is dedicated to the StreetSpace community of practice and the many young people whom we have shared this journey of discovery with. To Frontier Youth Trust who were probably the first to enter the Land of Dragons and continue to 'boldly go'.

Special thanks go to Debbie Garden and Nigel Pimlott for helping us edit the book and Indi who occupied herself for hours as we sought to meet the final deadline.

The world of young people can seem like a parallel universe – baffling and incomprehensible to older people. Richard Passmore's exploration of this territory starts with listening to young people themselves and reflecting on their insights through the perspective of Christian history and theology as well as the social sciences. The result is a fascinating account of the spirituality of youth culture and the opportunities presented for effective missional engagement – all of it grounded in the conviction that God is already at work out there, if only we have the eyes to see it.

John Drane and Olive Fleming Drane, authors, theologians and Affiliate Professors of Practical Theology at Fuller Seminary, California.

I've been waiting for this book since reading *Meet them where they're at* and it doesn't disappoint, exploring ways of finding shalom, missionally in places that need to be journeyed to with young people and beyond.

Alistair Jones, Chief Executive Officer, Frontier Youth Trust

This book is a theoretically complex, philosophically insightful, and intensely practical take on the dynamics of youth ministry. As such it is a rare contribution to the genre which tends to be dominated by 'how-to' pragmatics. Well done.

Alan Hirsch, award-winning author on missional Christianity and founder of Forge Mission Training Network. (alanhirsch.org)

An intelligent, challenging book that draws from Biblical and cultural expertise and hands-on experience to explore what Christian youth work needs to look like if it's going to reach beyond the doors of the church. Written by a man who desperately wants to see young people connect with the God who loves them so much, this is visionary, yet practical; resonant, yet radical... and it could transform the way you work with young people forever.

Martin Saunders, Editor of Youthwork magazine

Using the ancient mariner's imagery of dragons waiting off the end of the map, Passmore embraces this image as indicative of where youth work needs to go today. Furthermore, rather than respond with fear like the early sailors, Passmore encourages faith in a God who is big enough to take readers and youth workers into new places through leaving the current maps. ... For those who care about youth and wish to stay up with issues and trends from one who is both a thinker and practitioner, this is the book to read.

Dr. Rick Bartlett, Director of Theological Education – Tabor College, Kansas. Co-Author, Consuming Youth

A fine mix of story and critical reflection, this highly practical book provides a host of challenging insights, not just for Christian youth workers, but also for the church as a whole. A must-read for anyone who takes seriously the changing landscape of mission in Britain today.

Janet Sutton Webb, United Reform Church Pioneer Minister, Mid-Devon

This is a book I am so excited about. Richard helpfully assigns language and meaning to the thoughts and experiences of lots of youth workers who know that our methods, theories and theologies need to move on to meet the needs of the young people we seek to reach. It is likely to be a book that will provoke, irritate and challenge, but also one that will bring relief, encouragement, as well as practical ways forward to help us collapse the bridge between church and mission. I highly recommend this book, read it if you dare!

Jo Dolby, Youth Worker

Biographies

Richard Passmore has been described as one of the leading thinkers and practitioners around missional youth work and emerging church in the UK. He has worked for Frontier Youth Trust for over ten years, currently heading up StreetSpace, an initiative to explore what it means to grow church with young people from scratch, that has over forty linked in projects, engaging thousands of young people each week. He has spoken across Europe around the subjects of detached youth work and missional thinking, holds a Postgraduate Certificate in Practical Theology and is a qualified youth worker. Richard has written two previous books, *Meet them where they're at* and *Off the Beaten Track*, as well as numerous articles and papers, including the recently published Grove Booklet *Pioneer Youth Ministry* with Jo Dolby, and developed the *FaSt Game*, a unique way to help people engage and unpack the Christian story. He is married to Lorimer, has three children, and enjoys parties, food and kite flying.

Lorimer Passmore is a freelance writer and administrator. She has always had a passion for working with young people and has been involved in youth work as a volunteer since she was a teenager. She works as the administrator for the local StreetSpace project in Chard and wrote their '*Zine Training Manual* for young volunteers. She has a degree in Creative Writing and Drama from Bath Spa University College and has enjoyed all the learning she has had to do for this book! She has been married to Richard for nine years and loves to spend time with her daughter Indi and step-children Jo and Bethany. When she has the time she likes to squeeze in a bit of sewing, baking and walking along the lovely South West coast.

James Ballantyne is a detached youth worker for TheO6 project in Ottery St Mary, Devon. He is also a part-time lecturer for South West Youth Ministries and International Christian College, Glasgow (from where he graduated in 2008). For four years he coordinated the Sidewalk Project in Perth, Scotland where he participated in over four hundred sessions of detached youth work in different settings. He has youth work experience in churches and schools from his time in Perth and previously in Hartlepool. He is married to Lynn and has two children, he enjoys cycling, walking the dog, and is planning further study in detached youth work.

Contents

Foreword

Every now and again, a book comes along that stops you in your tracks. This is such a book. It will cause you to pause, reflect, unpack and re-think how you might go about Christian youth work and mission in the 21st century. For those who like an adventure, are looking for more relevant and appropriate ways of working with young people or are disturbed, frustrated or just bored with the sort of youth work currently on offer, this is a most excellent thing.

In simple terms this is a book about youth work, mission and church in the modern age. It is a book about exploration and discovery. The *Age of Discovery* took place between the 15th and 17th centuries, when intrepid explorers set off in search of unknown lands and peoples. During this period, map-makers had limited knowledge about the exact geography of our world. As new places were discovered, they were added to our knowledge of the known world and were mapped accordingly. However, much still remained unknown – and was thus literally considered 'off the map'.

The unknown places that were 'off the map' were often perceived as dangerous or mysterious and visually symbolised by sea serpents, mythological creatures or dragons. One historical map had the phrase 'Here be Dragons' written on it to mark the place at the edge of the known world. Richard and Lori have used this idea for the title of their book because it was an image that some of the people they work with felt best described the new missional landscape they were working in. They consider that mission with young people in the contemporary age is akin to the great exploratory journeys of old – full of unknowns, mystery, potential danger and accompanied by a myriad of exciting stories and remarkable discoveries.

This book reflects all these considerations. There is danger (especially if you like things as they are), mystery, hope and tales a-plenty of what happens when you trust God and set off into the unknown. In fact, there is something for everybody in this book. There are theoretical ideas, theological reflections, stories, practice ideas, practical solutions, wisdom, insight and experiences that all combine to produce a fast-moving book of journey and adventure.

Be in no doubt, this book will be a journey for those who dare to set sail and read it. It is not an easy read or a quick fix. It will require you to stop, think, reflect, respond and then press on some more. It will inspire, challenge and tease you and you will have to hold in tension numerous competing and potentially conflicting possibilities in order to reach the joys and riches of the new world.

I have known Richard and Lori for many years and am in a position to say that this is a book born out of lived experience and persistent dedication to young people and to seeking the Kingdom of God. The concepts described have arisen and then been polished by working with young people living real, messy, complicated, contradictory, exciting, and adventurous lives. Their proposals have then been sharpened as they have reflected upon what works. They have reflected upon how best to go about such work and are seeking, in this book, to convey the implications from their learning and experiences. The ideas in this book have been developed and honed by critical comments and suspicions from those who have had little desire to go 'off the map'. Richard and Lori want to tell their story and communicate the messages set out in this book to inspire and motivate other explorers who want to set sail into uncharted waters.

Having fully established their credentials for this work, I have to admit that I do not agree with all that they say in this book. This is not a criticism, but a positive reflection about the fact that working with young people can be mysterious and uncertain – anyone who tells you different is missing the point, has not done much youth work or is somewhat deluded! This reality demands new ideas and propositions in order to progress such work. It is a positive critique because it confirms that undertaking Christian-based youth work in the 21st century is not a 'done deal', but a wonderful exciting journey of discovery into an unknown land of working alongside God, following Her spirit, encountering young people and engaging the dragons that we might come across. Dilemmas will have to be faced, disagreements will abound, difficult decisions will have to be made and new possibilities will have to be considered. These scenarios sound just like those experienced by those brave and courageous explorers in the days of *The Age of Discovery* and those nervy, disorientated but spirit-filled disciples in the early church. I suggest they are dilemmas we need to embrace as we set sail in search of youth work and mission off the map. Enjoy!

Nigel Pimlott

Deputy Chief Executive Officer Frontier Youth Trust, co-author 'Youth Work After Christendom', 'Glimpses' and 'Glimpses for Young People'.

Preface: You Are Now Entering The 'Land of Dragons'

Ten years ago, when Richard originally wrote 'Meet them where they're at',[1] it was clear that we were in the midst of a big cultural shift in youth work and mission. Therefore, this book is more than an update of the original Meet them where they're at and will take readers beyond the map of their known world into the 'Land of Dragons'.

This land demands a radical shift in how we approach mission, church and youth work. This is necessary from a practical point of view (the world has changed), and a theological point of view (understandings of mission and church have changed). Like Meet them where they're at, this book draws on real stories of mission with young people in today's world, and goes deeper to consider new theological and practice ideas. We are still meeting young people where they're at and so what is offered here is what we have learnt so far on our continuing journey.

It is easier to stay where it is comfortable and familiar. It would be tempting to suggest either that change is not needed or that we simply 'tweak' what we are already doing. However, our continuing journey has convinced us that radical change is needed. If we are serious about undertaking mission with young people in the 21st century, we need to step out in faith to do something new. In so doing, we will discover God is already way ahead of us.

At the heart of this book we introduce the concept of 'Symbiotic Youth Work': a type of youth work where mission, church and young people are mutually dependent, in relationship with each other in a manner that is advantageous to everybody and where both youth worker and young person are treated equally. We argue that to reduce our way of being to a single component is to miss the heartbeat of what God is doing as He seeks to reconcile humanity and creation to Himself.

The mutual process of symbiosis made writing the book a challenge, as we needed to unpack some deep issues such as: What is church? What is mission? How do we think about, and even who is, God? We had to deconstruct a lot of what has gone before to reconstruct the mutual approach we have developed in Symbiotic Youth Work.

At times we will ask you to hold several competing ideas in your head as we unpack: how we got to where we are today; the reasons why we need to change; and what that change looks like in practice. However the Christian story is one rooted in hope – hope for a better future and the hope that we can find ways to help young people connect meaningfully with God and the community around them. What we offer in this book are real stories of hope from our journey off the edge of the map, as God meets young people where they're at.

We have split the book into four sections: In Section 1 we introduce the idea of 'Flow' and explore the theological background and rationale for why we do what we do as we journey to *The Edge of the Map* and beyond into the Land of Dragons.

In Section 2 we consider some *Resources for the Road*. We explore why we shouldn't fear stepping out into the unknown. We consider how our practice should be shaped by clear values and the core principles of youth work rather than by externally determined targets and agendas. We analyse the genetics of Symbiotic Youth Work and explain why we think this innovative approach to youth work is paramount to the survival of the church. In order to increase understanding about the nature of 'symbiosis in practice' we have included short reflections throughout the book as we seek to re-imagine church and community in the Land of Dragons.

Section 3, entitled *Stepping Out*, includes a detailed analysis of the Nine-Stage Process used by all StreetSpace projects. This was included in the original *Meet them where they're at*, but has been revised and updated for this book. Whilst many of the stories and examples used are from detached work, you will also find stories from other youth work contexts. The Nine Stages discussed in Section 3, though primarily considered from a detached youth work perspective, can equally be applied to open youth clubs or youth drop-in centres. Where the Stages need adaptation, this is specified.

Section 4, *Base Camp*, addresses the more practical aspects of youth and community work, such as community profiling, project management, and monitoring and evaluation. Again, many of examples are from a detached work context, but the lessons can equally be applied to all work in the Land of Dragons.

Throughout the book, we have included short sections entitled, *Symbiosis in Practice* to highlight the key themes or ideas presented in each section or chapter.

Richard and Lori Passmore

Section 1:
The Edge of the Map

Chapter 1 – The Story So Far

Greetings from the church of 'Flow'

In the beginning there was Flow, and the Flow was God and God created the heavens and the earth. The earth was formless and empty, and darkness covered the deep waters, and God's Flow was hovering over the surface of the waters. As God created the light His Flow was present, both in the darkness of night and the lightness of day.

As the waters separated, Flow was all around. It ebbed and surged with the waves and the tides of the seas. At the creation of the land, Flow was in the soil and the solid rock, in the dust and in the sand, in the darkest depths of the landmass, and on the surface of the land that was bathed in light.

So that this creation itself might grow and learn to join the Flow, God gave the sun to nourish the creation and moon to increase and govern the tides and make the whole world flow in His likeness.

God's Flow was so embedded in the land that it came to breathe, in colours and textures, Flow inhabited every leaf, and root and plant. And because the seas were bubbling with God's Flow, they too sprung to life, and these creations knew the Flow. So these creatures inhabited the sea and the land, and when their feet were rooted in the soil or the water, they were rooted in Flow. All these many kinds of living and flowing animals, birds and insects, creatures large and small, Flow created.

Finally God said, "Let us create humanity. They will have Flow within them like us and live in the earth".

The idea of 'Flow' is very important in seeking to understand Symbiotic Youth Work. The stories of Flow evolved from our work with a group of young people who use the local skate park where we live in Chard, Somerset. Approximately a year and a half after we first contacted the group through detached youth work sessions, we went with them on a skate and bike pilgrimage. We had formed relationships with a core group of young people who had little knowledge of Christianity and what they did know was mainly gleaned from school or television programmes. The pilgrimage was an opportunity to develop relationships with them and begin to challenge them about life, spirituality and the world within the framework of a well-established, mutually accepted relationship between the leaders and the young people.

The idea of going on a trip, calling it a 'pilgrimage' and telling stories was developed with the young people. They were involved in the whole process, from the initial concept to the more practical elements. Many youth workers know the importance of enabling young people to shape what happens in a youth project. At a practical level this is fairly straightforward. For example, this might involve enabling young people to plan the menu, do the shopping or cooking and other practical matters. However, this pilgrimage was rooted in the fact the young people not only worked on the practicalities but also on the very concept.

The whole idea of pilgrimage was new to the young people, but it fitted into the broader journey that both the young people and the workers were on; namely, discovering what it means to be and grow church in today's context. Using the language of pilgrimage and developing together what we meant by this, we unfolded what it meant to be community, reciprocally with the young people. This sense of being on a mutual journey of discovery with young people is at the heart of this book. We hope you will journey through the stories with us and similarly be able to unfold community and church with the young people you work with.

Throughout the book we will use the words 'church' and 'community' interchangeably. As you continue reading, you will discover why this is. Our journey has made us explore the importance of youth work, youth work's roots in mission and what the values that underpin youth work mean in practice. It has also raised questions about church and culture. This book will perhaps ask more questions than it offers answers. For example, how do you connect with a group of young people around the idea of God and how can you be church with those young people, on their terms, where they are? It was out of these types of questions that the notion of 'Flow' evolved: moments of young people seeing G-d in their own culture through their own eyes.

When skating or biking, the young people we were working with experienced a oneness with their boards or bikes – a moment in time – something they called 'Flow'. So together, with that expression and that connection, we created a story; one rooted in a Christian tradition that they could not only understand, but also participate in.

We saw no mass conversions and no dramatic increase in the numbers of young people attending church in Chard. What we

1

shared in was the birth of what we called the 'Church of Flow'. We were growing church/community with the young people, accepting that this may be transient, temporary, and defined through the process of journey. As workers we were setting out to discover what church/community is in today's culture, through intentionally trying to be and grow church/community WITH young people. This was the beginning of a journey that has seen the emergence of the national StreetSpace detached youth work movement. As a result, this book is not only able to draw on the story of a single project or piece of work, but on stories and learning from a community of projects working in different settings (rural, urban, suburban, with different tribes of young people in different contexts) and uses these connections and stories to explore what being and growing new forms of church/community means in practice, simultaneously considering some of the theological implications of this.

A changing landscape

Since the publication of *Meet them where they're at* in 2003, the landscape of both youth work and mission has changed dramatically. Statutory youth service budgets have been drastically cut and many communities around the UK have seen their Local Authority youth centre closed. Where once there were many youth workers engaging with local young people, now there are often only one or two workers covering a wide geographical area – if you are lucky. This ever-changing sphere of youth work has seen an increase in charitable, non-profit organisations and even businesses stepping into the youth work breach to try and patch up the gaps left by a retreating statutory youth service. For example, the StreetSpace community have discovered that the way we develop church/community is so rooted and well grounded in the core values of youth and community work that local councils, funders, and communities embrace many of our projects. In Section Four we show some of the ways that StreetSpace is leading the sector in measuring and evaluating progress and outcomes with young people.

Equally there have been many changes in the role and language of church and mission, such as the growth of Fresh Expressions, Emerging Church, and Pioneer Ministry Training. We will explore some of these changes later. The implications of this shifting role of the church in our communities are a central theme of this book, and a valuable resource from which we can learn. This leads us back to 'Flow' and the need to start viewing 'church' and 'youth work' in radically different ways if we are going to play our part in the new landscape. We hope that the stories written in this book will inspire and challenge you to discover your place on the map and start (or continue) a journey to a new place.

This book has been several years in the making. During that time, the StreetSpace community of practice has been established and developed – there are now forty-one projects across the UK which contact over seven thousand young people each week. It has been a journey – a personal one, a communal one, and a shifting one – embracing the various changes and challenges that today's society brings. However, it is a journey that builds on a rich history, that seeks to explore, unpack and guide you through youth work and mission within this new context that we find ourselves. Frontier Youth Trust (FYT), the charity behind StreetSpace, has an established reputation for engaging in cutting edge, pioneering ministry. FYT's strap line is: 'mission with young people at risk'. This is FYT's ethic and core motivation. FYT serves to empower and bring about justice with young people, and to equip those working with young people on the margins of church and society through resourcing and training youth workers.

FYT has a history of pioneering practice and as such has always supported *edgy youth work* and mission – both practically and theologically. Much of the background theology of 'Kingdom Shalom', or God leading humanity towards wholeness through Jesus, came from the first FYT resident theologian, Jim Punton. The effects of his work have been far reaching and impacted much of the youth ministry and church we see at work today, in the UK and beyond.[i]

We need to keep central the idea that it is Jesus who shapes our mission, which shapes our church, which, in turn, informs our future. Not the other way around. In Christ we see the bringing of renewal and this is our hope for the future; a renewed earth and heaven, not earth as a Titanical ship set to sink. In the Lord's Prayer we pray, "… your kingdom come, your will be done, on earth as it is in heaven" (Matthew 6:10), and we need to recognise that we live in this *in-between time*, that the Kingdom is both now and not yet. Theologians talk about this as our 'eschatological hope'[ii] and it is this hope for the Kingdom's presence here on earth that shapes our thinking in the Land of Dragons.

---

[i] See www.fyt.org.uk for some of Jim's papers and Pete Ward's *Growing up Evangelical* regarding the impact youth ministry has had on the wider church. Jim was also on the original planning groups for Greenbelt and was one of the first Greenbelt speakers.

[ii] One writer who explores this further is N. T. Wright particularly in his book *Surprised by Hope: Rethinking Heaven, the Resurrection, and the Mission of the Church*.

Method actors immerse themselves in the character they are playing so that at any moment they can draw on their preparation in order to improvise a scene in character. Like such an actor, we need to invest time in prayer, in being in community, in spiritual awareness and in silence, so we are suitably anchored in this hope for the journey ahead. If we invest time in the spiritual virtues and become part of the Flow, we are ready at any given moment to respond to the unfolding Kingdom. It becomes second nature to move in the new landscape with G-d and others towards a more hopeful future.

God and G-d

You will have seen that we use different terms for God. 'God' is the familiar word used in the Bible, church and for liturgy. 'G-d' is used in the Hebraic tradition where, out of reverence and respect afforded to G-d, His name is not fully written down. This suggests the mystery of G-d; that he can never be fully known.

You will see we have used different written forms in different places in this book, according to the context that we are discussing at the time. For example, we might write 'God' when we are talking about how He is viewed by traditional church. We might use the term 'G-d' in relation to a project that is trying to work out who G-d is in the Land of Dragons; the G-d that we can never fully comprehend.

The StreetSpace story

StreetSpace came into being as a result of the changing landscape and language around Church. The growth of the alternative worship movement had been helpful – but from an FYT perspective – raised questions about how *missional* it was and if it was sufficient to reach more marginalised communities. Therefore in partnership with Jonny Baker at Church Missionary Society (CMS), a leading exponent of emerging church, StreetSpace was established. The basic principle was to ask: 'What can missional youth work learn from the emerging church and what can the emerging church learn from missional youth work?' StreetSpace was piloted in three areas: a rural setting on the edge of Dartmoor in Devon; a city context in Birmingham; and a market town in Somerset. The project was deliberately positioned to hold in tension the values of modern youth work practice (education, equality, participation and empowerment) and a missional approach, rooted in Christian values and principles.

Richard Passmore set up what was originally called 'Chard detached youth work project' with one volunteer in 2006. Through regular weekly contact with young people out on the streets, the project started to build relationships with a core group of young people down at the local skate park. The project was able to fundraise with the young people to improve the skate park, engage them in consultation about town planning, discuss national youth work cuts and take them on trips and residentials exploring with them the message of Flow.

This work further expanded over time to include meals and meetings, also known as 'M&Ms': a creative way of connecting young people with their wider community. Written up by a leading think tank[i] as a model of good practice, M&Ms also facilitates meetings with a core group of young people over the winter months when it is cold and dark and they are less likely to be found out and about on the streets. The Chard group meets once a month at a local Indian restaurant and plans trips, offers feedback on plans and continues to build relationships.

M&Ms is an emerging process and has gone through several incarnations. For a while it became 'Curry Church' as the second generation of young people involved in the project started to explore Flow in a new way. More recently it has become a core community/church gathering point for the third generation of young people involved. The lessons learnt in Chard were put to good use and in April 2010 'StreetSpace National' was born and rolled out across the UK. Since then, this community of practitioners, youth workers and volunteers has grown, developed and learnt from one another.

All StreetSpace projects work to a Nine-Stage Process originally created when Richard worked for Youth for Christ in Cheltenham in the early 1990s. It is building on and adapting this model that has helped develop a broader theological and practical understanding of what it means to be and grow church/community with young people. In many ways, young people themselves have been central in developing the StreetSpace approach. The process is outlined in more detail in Section 3 of this book.

StreetSpace does not force anyone to adopt a particular model of working, but offers a development tool and process to help meet young people where they're at and grow church with young people on the edge of society as a missionary endeavour. The process is a framework that can facilitate locally grounded and 'resource-lite' youth work projects and expressions of church, **if** the young people

---

i See Demos report, '*A scoping study concerning community empowerment issues relating to children and young people*' (2009). A copy of their report can be found on the FYT website www.fyt.org.uk.

1

wish to journey in this way.[i]

We talk about young people self-determining the outcomes of a project whilst retaining the desire to be rigorous and open in our approach to youth work and non-dualistic in our approach to mission and G-d. Symbiotic Youth Work is an experiment in cultural mission, which holds humility as a core value, alongside a desire to learn from those we are engaging with. There is a mutual relationship between the worker and the young people and it is this mutuality, this journeying together, that is at the very heart of what StreetSpace is all about. At a time when both the notion of 'church' and the connotations surrounding this notion are often negative, restrictive and prescriptive, it is a reimagining of what community, informed by Shalom principles, could be.

StreetSpace uses an action research approach[ii] to discover how un-churched young people would define, develop and shape church together. This is undertaken with youth workers as they move through the Nine Stages, developing culturally relevant expressions of church, infused with a sense of community. Over time, it became evident there was a need to update *Meet them where they're at* to encompass this idea in a way which sought to build on the rich tradition of missional youth work, thus bringing together the learning from the emerging cultural context and shifting theological paradigm now present.

Brian McLaren, a well-known American exponent of the emerging church, has talked about traditional divisions and doctrinal differences giving way to a new focus on God and the story of God's love for this world.[2] This book has been written to be read within the context of this new landscape and the emerging, missional context and story we find ourselves in. We hope you will feel the contours of the new land and step into this new place so that the familiar story will echo back to you in a new way.

Navigating in the Land of Dragons

One of the questions we often ask in StreetSpace training is, "Have you ever been on a residential or at a youth work event where you instinctively felt 'this is what church is really about?'" – that moment when things seem to really come together and the group is more than just the sum of its parts; when you know there is something

---

[i] These expressions of church all look very different from one another and examples are given later in the book.
[ii] Reflection is undertaken about what is done with young people in particular settings in order to improve practice, understanding and the situations young people find themselves in.

1

distinct and holy happening but do not have the language to describe it. Similarly, 'Here Be Dragons' is an image beyond our imagination, beyond church and beyond youth work, but still a place where G-d dwells and where the Holy Spirit will lead. This metaphorical image offers us scope to explore what it means to journey into new territories alongside young people. In using this metaphor, we are not saying that the young people are 'dragons'; rather that we should 'boldly go' into a new land. We offer this book as a navigational guide to a place that, although sometimes uncomfortable or dangerous, is still a place you choose to journey to. This Land of Dragons analogy has been helpful in verbalising or imagining the space we (and an increasing number of youth workers and emerging church practitioners) find ourselves in.

Unlike a map, which is fixed and shows us identifiable landmarks, we find ourselves in a landscape that is continually culturally shifting. The wind and water continually change the landscape of the six hundred square miles of sand dunes at the Lençóis Maranhenses National Park, in Brazil. Similarly, we find ourselves in a continually shifting context and culture.

So how do we negotiate this new and unknown terrain? There are many different tools you can use to aid your journey. The first tool you need for the journey is a compass. This compass has the specific purpose of helping you navigate the new landscape. Unlike a traditional compass, however, this one only has three points to it – representing the directions of the *Bible*, *Tradition* and *Culture* as illustrated in figure 1.[i]

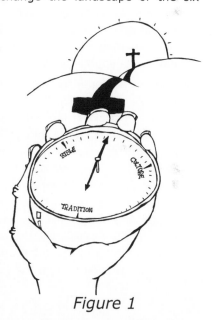

Figure 1

The idea behind this compass is that our direction of travel will be informed by reference to these three points as we seek to navigate our way into the unknown. The *Bible* offers us a narrative that we can use on our journey. We can draw upon its wisdom for encouragement, allow it to inform our values and morals and use it to challenge us in our work. *Tradition* is about learning from the rich

---

[i] For a further study about these three directional points, see Grenz and Franke (2001).

1

heritage of Christianity that previous travellers have taught us. This includes, for example, learning from the different ways we have learnt to pray and worship over the centuries, various rituals and approaches to the major Christian festivals. *Culture* is all around us. Its influences are far reaching, from the clothes we choose to wear to the political beliefs we hold. In any given situation, we can allow the Spirit of G-d to direct us by seeking guidance from these three reference points. Thus, at different times on our journey, the compass might point us in a particular direction.

Sometimes the compass may guide us in a more *Bible* direction. For example, we might take a Bible story and re-imagine it with the young people in contemporary culture. The *culture* of the young people might demonstrate the Kingdom in action. For example, it is often part of youth culture to show a high level of commitment to friends and a strong sense of community. Alternatively we may swing more towards *tradition* perhaps sharing communion with the young people, although maybe using cola and cake rather than bread and wine! Moving with G-d in the direction the compass points helps us to take the opportunities to unfold the now and not yet Kingdom with young people.

Just like a traditional compass, ours is also influenced by a magnetic force: the guiding power of the missio Dei,[i] our true North. As we follow the missio Dei into the new landscape She will be there to guide and navigate us. Although sometimes the needle may lead us in one particular direction, we must hold this in tension with the other points on the compass to ensure that we do not allow one particular point to completely dominate and blow us off course. All three navigational points have a role to play in discovering the new landscape and we should be wary of straying too far in any one direction to the exclusion of the other points. We will further explore this idea later on in the book but at this juncture, we identify the compass as the first tool for the journey.

Symbiosis in Practice

What has been highlighted is that the two concepts of 'church' and 'community' are much more closely linked than we could have imagined, and the first tool for the journey is the compass that will help you navigate the new landscape.

---

[i] Or Mission of G-d, sending of G-d.

Chapter 2 – Unpacking the Landscape

Finding our way

In this chapter, we will refer to the 'maps' that are familiar to us. These are maps we have grown up with and that have influenced our approach, theology and culture. They have given us our current understanding of the foundations and history of the church and society. We will also explore the techniques and tools needed for the journey into the Land of Dragons, unpacking what a new approach to youth work and mission might look like and how best we can implement this.

> When Moses sent them [the spies] off to scout out Canaan, he said, "Go up through the Negev and then into the hill country. Look the land over, see what it is like. Assess the people: Are they strong or weak? Are there few or many? Observe the land: Is it pleasant or harsh? Describe the towns where they live: Are they open camps or fortified with walls? And the soil: Is it fertile or barren? Are there forests? And try to bring back a sample of the produce that grows there—this is the season for the first ripe grapes."
> **Numbers 13:17-20, The Message**

Rather like Joshua and Caleb (two of the spies sent by Moses), we find ourselves scouting out new territory, looking for the Promised Land. Expectantly, we search through our binoculars to try and gain a better understanding of the place we will soon be entering. We take note of the terrain: the contours, green spaces, mountains, rivers and other distinguishing features. We are also wary of what we might encounter and perhaps nervous about what dangers await us. All the time, we know that we will have to discover for ourselves what lies ahead. If we simply observe and do not actually enter we will never know what is in the land. Our observations will help us decide how to best equip ourselves for our onward journey.

When going on an expedition in centuries past people would load up pack animals and take an extensive army of servants with all the equipment required – it was not exactly travelling light! It was an age of empire building and conquest. In these next two chapters, we explore the tools you will need for your journey into the Land of Dragons: a streamlined list of tools and equipment to assist you in your quest of discovery rather than conquest. In this section we explore the edges of the known map and what we already know about living in a post-Christian, post-modern context, preparing ourselves to venture off the map.

1

A year after starting detached work in Chard, we decided it was a good time to consolidate the group and so we decided to go on a skate safari visiting several skate parks around the county.

The weather was great and getting lost in the minibus on the way to the first park just gave it that edgy feel that we were on more than just a 'trip'. Arriving at Ilchester Skate Park, the group piled out – after memorising the First Rule of Skate Safari: 'If you break your neck, it's not our fault!'

We had picked several parks to travel around. I was driving and various young people helped with navigating – that allowed conversations to happen. As we drove on to Weston-Super-Mare, I started chatting to one of the lads helping me navigate. "How does it feel when you skate and everything is going great?" I asked. "It's like you're one with your board." He replied. "Is it spiritual?" I countered. "Yeah, the adrenaline is going and you just flow". "I think that's God, but you don't have the language to call it that." I replied.

We chatted some more about how this must be similar to how a surfer feels at one with the world when 'in the zone'. The conversation got round to the idea of doing a skate church and my experiences of doing church on the streets with young people. After giving me a few strange looks, they got the idea. I talked to them about doing a skate pilgrimage, which they were very excited about, and we continued chatting about old Celtic saints and crosses around Cornwall they had seen. We decided that a nutty Celtic saint would be a good patron for skaters.

Later in the trip I had the opportunity to chat to a couple more of the young people about skating and spirituality. They talked about different experiences, about the process of coming up with a new trick and how it feels to perfect it.

Eight and a half hours later we were exhausted, everyone had a battle scar or burn to take away as their memento of the day, but everyone had remembered the First Rule of Skate Safari and no one had broken their neck!

Richard Passmore

This was one of the first trips with the young people and we were pleased we had framed it as a 'safari'. It built on the idea that we were exploring with young people. Looking back it is hard to say if it was a young person or a worker who first suggested the 'safari' terminology, such was the pace of the conversation. Regardless, it defined the nature of the trip and introduced early on a language of space and of movement that could be developed.

Working in a post-Christendom era

Post-Christendom is the edge of the known map: it is the place we currently stand on the boundary of our known and unknown worlds. For some, standing here fills them with fear and trepidation whilst for others excitement and adrenaline and perhaps curiosity or scepticism pervade. This is the place where our preparation begins. It acknowledges what we already know, and starts to explore the new, just like Joshua and Caleb did when they set out on their journey.

We will now explore what it means to live in a post-Christendom and post-evangelism context, considering the role of 'tradition' in our approach to missional work with young people. In *Youth Work After Christendom*[3] the authors explore what it means to engage in youth work in this new context. They suggest that church attendance among young people is on the decline and that, whilst Christianity began as a radical, subversive and underground movement, it has since developed into a more established, institutional form typified by many churches today.

Referencing Stuart Murray's book *Post-Christendom*, they contend that as the new post-Christendom culture emerges, Christianity loses its influence within society today. What was once a powerful and influential belief system does not now seem to speak to current generations in the way it once did. They go on to list the following, illustrating the movement from Christendom to a post-Christendom era.[4]

- Christianity is moving away from the centre of society to the edge;
- Christians are moving away from being a majority to a minority, and therefore losing the influence they once had;
- Where previously Christians found themselves embedded in the world where they shaped culture, now they find themselves outsiders, exiles in an unfamiliar culture;
- In Christendom Christians were privileged, in post-Christendom they find themselves just one of many elements in a pluralistic society;
- In Christendom Christians sought to control society, now they can only influence through witness of their story;
- We are moving away from a position of Christians

17

1

> maintaining what they have and towards becoming more missional in approach; and
>
> - We are moving from being institutionalised to being a movement, as seen in the early days of Christianity.

Over the years, we as youth workers have all built up a kit bag of tools that have helped us in our work with young people. However, we may be like the explorers of long ago, carrying tools that had once been useful but are now no longer fit for purpose in the post-Christendom era. Some of these trusty tools (such as a book of creative Bible studies, which assume that people know the basic stories), might prove ineffective in this new landscape and instead of being of benefit may actually weigh us down. For example, when going on an expedition to the arctic, an ice pick and crampons might be vital for the journey, but would be rendered useless in a desert. It is not that these tools do not have value, but they may not be suitable for the environments we might find ourselves in. Remember, we are not like the explorers of old, seeking to build an empire. We must lose our Christendom-orientated tools to make room for the new ones relevant in the Land of Dragons.

A large part of what we carry with us is rooted in our own spirituality. Spirituality as a concept can be difficult to pin down. It has different meanings for different races, peoples and cultures. Our own view of spirituality might be different to that of the young people we work with.[i]

At a recent gathering of StreetSpace workers, the following thoughts were offered on what spirituality was: beyond self; connecting with the 'other' or a 'supreme being'; the unknown deep within; feeling worthy; other faith groups; awe; being transformed; it's reflective, active, personal and communal; nature; being fully human but not humanistic; and restoration of humanity.

Much of what we think in the west is influenced by Greek philosophy and the pursuit of truth. The role of argument and debate, the use of logic as the tool to understanding and learning stems from the Greek philosophers Socrates, Plato and Aristotle. This gives insight into how we as a western culture think: we use a process of 'distilling' (i.e. separating something out into component parts so that we understand it more) to help us to achieve meaning. The way we think is a bit like a purification process which filters out the bits that are not relevant through questioning and dialogue. At one level there is nothing wrong with this because it enables us to analyse and

---

[i] For a further discussion about spirituality, see Bullock and Pimlott (2008).

consider the different points of an argument. It also helps us make our own decisions based on our personal knowledge and other resources available to us. However, it potentially limits our understanding as we can easily get caught up with the idea that we need to filter out the bits we don't like or understand, rather than seeing things from a completely different perspective.[i] For example, historically we have tended to be locked into thinking about church on a Sunday and will change the way we do Sunday services to increase their appeal, rather than re-thinking church as a concept. This is particularly the case with spirituality. If we compare this western 'argument' based approach, to a more eastern perspective that holds the tension between different ideas, recognising mystery and more holistic approaches, we see the beginnings of a different way of approaching issues, people and cultures.

With the rise of theology as an academic discipline and people thinking more critically around Christian spirituality, we have seen the development of different theological typologies. Typologies are often used in social sciences and theology as a way of grouping different themes within a subject area. If we are going to use our compass and use the direction that *tradition* may pull us in, it is helpful to understand how that tradition has informed mission and church through the ages. Bevans and Schroeder[5] helpfully outline six questions they say are always present when thinking about mission and the church:

1. Who is Jesus Christ and what is his meaning?
2. What is the nature of the Christian church?
3. How does the church regard its eschatological future (addressing the end of the world prophesy)?
4. What is the nature of the salvation it preaches?
5. How does the church value the human?
6. What is the value of human culture as the context in which the gospel is preached?

Church history and tradition have left us with a number of clearly identifiable strands of theological thinking that have shaped contemporary mission and practice. For example, there is the tradition that regards personal salvation as the key purpose in God's mission. Alternatively, there is the typology that focuses upon humanity as a whole, where the seeking of truth and enlightenment for universal benefit is the mission. Furthermore, there is a typology

---

[i] For a further reading, see De Bono (1995).

1

that considers freedom and liberation from injustice to be the driver behind mission. There is also a strand, based upon Catholic Social Teaching, that emphasises the significance of humanity and a quest for the common good as God's missional imperative. There are also more recent *traditions* that have shaped thinking and impacted mission and understanding. For example, there are the traditions that emphasise black theology and civil rights, feminist interpretations and perspectives, charismatic and Pentecostal strands, the radical orthodoxy view and liberal and post-modern perspectives. All these *traditions* or types have influenced how we undertake mission, facilitate church and view humanity, the end times and the cultural context we find ourselves in.

These constants and typologies offer us points of reference as we seek to unfold a new way of being church with young people. They are potentially helpful in understanding how our contemporary beliefs have developed. However, they are often rooted in a western thought process. If we are living in a post-Christendom era, we see ourselves moving into a time of fluidity and movement. Christianity is no longer at the centre of the map, with its well established landmarks, routes and contours. We are at the edge of the map; a place with no definable borders. Everything is blurred and we find ourselves as nomads, wanderers and migrants in an unfamiliar land. In order to exist within this new space, we have to liberate ourselves from being defined by any one particular historical typology. Instead, we need to learn from tradition and take this learning with us into the new land to discover fresh understanding.

If we align ourselves too fully to any one particular typology, we could miss out on what G-d is already doing in the community. We could too easily end up like the colonial explorers of old, bringing our understood version of *the truth* to people in perceived need, rather than genuinely walking alongside people like Jesus did. Richard recounts his own journey to illustrate this point:

> *After years of living on and working in a challenging housing estate, a disconnect between the approach of the churches working on the estate and the people of the estate became apparent: the churches sought to save people from a perceived dark place, when in reality I encountered G-d every day on the streets and with my neighbours. This is not to say there was not darkness present, but there was a growing recognition of G-d's presence on the estate, evidencing the reality that the Kingdom is definitely now, as well as not yet. The churches surrounding the estate did not have a monopoly*

on G-d – She was active and real on the street.
Richard Passmore

Therefore we want you to read this book with an uncluttered mind, one free of fixed influences and suggestions. You may find this difficult to do. You might not always agree with the direction we are travelling. We hope, however, that you will still engage with the process. So leave your 'concept' of God at home, see what G-d is doing and, to quote one member of the StreetSpace team, "Do the stupid thing".

Feeling our way

In order to better prepare ourselves to follow the missio Dei we need to break free of the constricted western way of thinking and find new ways of engaging. If we go back to the Jewish roots of Christianity, we find a way of being that fits more with the processes we are considering. It is living out, engaging in and wading into the messy stuff that is important, not just trying to bring *a truth* to a situation or even trying to journey to a fixed destination. There is a sense that we are 'all in this together', in a place where all are able to contribute, to engage, to be and do. This is difficult for us to comprehend because of our ingrained western approach that is rooted in individualism and notions of a 'fixed truth'. Rabbi Jonathan Sacks argues that Judaism embraces diversity whereas Christianity searches for universal truths. [6]

Sometimes we have to 'feel it' as well as 'think it'. We have to do what is in front of us. There will be the desire to define matters, to make sense of things, but we want to encourage a 'letting go' as you respond to the leading of the Spirit and follow the missio Dei into the Land of Dragons. This can be frightening, but it can also be liberating and exhilarating. We are not giving you a formula, any pre-determined structure or absolute imperatives, but an invitation to follow the compass and let it guide you as you see the needle point towards the relevant path. This is not to imply the journey will have an absence of values; these are required to guide your good practice. The Nine-Stages discussed later in this book are such a guide (rather than a strategy with defined timelines), and something to help you remain a pilgrim in the new land, not just become a settler.

A good way to explain what we mean is to ask you to imagine you are climbing a mountain. You could just stand at the bottom look up, examine from the ground and wait for something to happen. Although thinking and planning are essential for your journey it is

1

'feeling' your way that will help you progress. At some point you will have to connect with the rock in front of you, to engage with it, to feel for suitable crevices with your fingers and your feet so you can anchor yourself to the rock face. You must feel your way as well as think about it. You continue to climb, feeling your way as you go. It will be slow at times, you may find yourself going sideways or down before you go up. At points you may think you have found a good route, but when you traverse along it you may see that it doesn't offer all the promise you thought it did. You cannot see the summit and you may never reach the top. But it is this 'feeling' as well as the 'thinking' that will assist you on your journey. We will explore some of the practicalities of 'feeling' your way later when we introduce the concept of 'tacking'.

So how do we ground this borderless spirituality? Firstly, we must move into this new context. It can be difficult to have one foot within a new way of being and the other in 'church' that is traditional in its perspectives. Moving in fully may require us to make some sacrifices. For example, at a recent StreetSpace gathering some workers discussed that, when setting out into the unknown without destination, they had worried about their own children's spiritual journeys. They said they had wrestled with whether they should take their children to a traditional church to give them a grounded start to their Christian faith. We are aware that by going on this new and unknowable journey we may have to sacrifice the conventional way our children's spirituality develops in pursuit of a new way.

How we use language is very important in our journey. We want to redeem words like 'church' and 'prayer'. As we unfold what these words mean in the Land of Dragons, we discover their meaning deepens and expands. For example, one detached work team took a small leather book with them when going out on the streets. They would ask the young people if they would like the team to pray for them and they would write these prayer requests in the little book. They didn't shy away from using the word 'prayer' and were never met with hostility but rather curiosity; the young people would share their prayers or not as they wished. What unfolded for this team was an exciting journey to a new place and understanding about what prayer was. Their full story is included later in this book.

Understand that you will have a mediation role, partnering with God. We are the story-bringers and cannot get away from this. Nevertheless, we need to find new ways to bring the story. The old tools may no longer work. As Christians and human 'becomings', we are both convinced of the story and still exploring the story.

However, this can all too easily create inertia if we are too precious about the past and fail to risk releasing the story in a new way. If you stand on the precipice of a ravine but do not shout, you will never hear an echo. If you shout at a wall, you will still hear no echo. We want you to engage in a process of calling out and listening for what the echo sounds like. Working in this way means we tell the story and learn from how it is understood so that we 'become' together with the young people we are engaging. This is what often happened in the early church. For example, the early disciples predominantly had a Jewish culture and background. As they went on their journey they, perhaps inevitably, called out from their Jewish perspective. However, the echo came back in non-Jewish language, customs and practices. The gospel took on new understandings and meanings – Peter's vision and conversation with God about eating 'unclean' foods in Acts 10 is a good illustration of this. In a similar way, we need to recognise who we are and what we bring into the public space, feeling our way and co-creating with the young people and community we encounter in the new land.

Embracing dissent

Much of what we are suggesting is designed to bring about change and promote dissent, as we become catalysts for change. Gerald Arbuckle[7] advocates dissent, as without dissent within an organisation or church, it might not evolve. Dissent helps suggest new, innovative ways of doing things to give longevity and new life. It offers movement to a static and shrinking institution. In our context, it is about offering alternatives. Unfortunately, new ideas are often vulnerable and can be easily squashed before they have even had a chance to get established. Churches often maintain the status quo and dissent might be needed to offer creative alternatives and new ways of thinking. These new ideas might be seen as chaotic and something that disturbs the equilibrium. This can cause confusion, anger, and a 'pulling of ranks' as old ways are jealously protected. Dissenters are often marginalised because they do not toe the line, or fit in with the dominant culture. Jesus was a dissenter.

Arbuckle goes on to talk about two types of dissenters: 'authority dissenters' and 'pathfinding dissenters'.[8] Here we will look at the role both of these have in reimagining church. Authority dissenters are those in appointed leadership positions who adopt a 'transforming' style, opening up for others dramatic new ways of doing things. Pathfinder dissenters are those who dream things can be different and just get on with being that difference.

1

It is the role of good authority dissenters to hold many things in tension. They are proactive and empowering people who recognise change has to happen. They explore opportunities for change, whilst being aware some people will reflexively resist change. They help give shape to, and communicate the vision for community growth to others and develop strategies that allow vision to come to fruition. Good transforming leaders will live out this vision themselves: it needs to be authentic. They will recognise the need for creative innovators to instigate change whilst also ensuring these innovators are accountable for their behaviour. Good leaders 'own' their authority, not for stamping over everything in a negative fashion, but rather recognising the requirement that they 'lead', even if it means upsetting some people along the way.

Change has to happen. As Arbuckle radically asserts, you need to "innovate or die".[9] We know through the work StreetSpace is participating in nationally that change is necessary. It isn't easy and there are many struggles along the way. Responsible dissenters are needed for change to happen but often, as is seen throughout culture and society, people don't like change. Change causes anxiety and a knee jerk reaction often results to protect 'what is' rather than embrace the change.

Examples of good authority dissenters are Steve Chalke[i] (who recently wrote an article challenging the attitudes around gay marriage), and Graham Cray,[ii] who has been instrumental in promoting new ways of being and doing church.

Sometimes in our work it is necessary for authority and pathfinding dissenters to work together. A good example of this type of partnership can be seen in one of our local projects where a church, with a mainly aging congregation, appointed a part-time youth worker.

> As an authority dissenter, the minister of the church approached his managers and insisted that funding, which his managers had set aside for something else, be used to support a youth club. His managers knew StreetSpace worked in the area so only offered to consider funding the youth club if the church was willing to work with StreetSpace. StreetSpace workers, as pathway dissenters, only agreed to work with the church if they could have the freedom to grow something new

---

[i] See www.christianitymagazine.co.uk/sexuality/stevechalke.aspx

[ii] Graham Cray is The Archbishops' Missioner and Team Leader of Fresh Expressions, a role that focuses on how the Gospel connects with contemporary culture and the theology of renewal.

in the Land of Dragons, rather than just set up a youth club.

A group of young people wanted to explore their questions about faith. They were keen to use the church building, rather than the hall the youth club met in. However, the large space was cold and slightly intimidating. Therefore the youth worker decided a good use of space would be to put up a gazebo inside the church to explore together what it means to find G-d and be church. This caused some upset because of the original congregation's protective attitude towards the church building. The youth worker, as a pathfinding dissenter, did not go out of her way to upset people, but was not afraid to challenge the attitudes and perceptions the original congregation had about their church in order to facilitate the appropriate space for the young people.

Work is undertaken to explore spirituality in the gazebo as this is a unique shared space between the church and the young people. Because the group are all from non-church backgrounds, and the values of the workers are rooted in mutuality and joint discovery, there is a great relationship with the established church. However, it is only because the authority dissenter gives the space for the worker, and does not require the young people to conform to traditional patterns of church, that something beautiful is being brought to life.
Anonymous

Pathfinding dissenters are gifted with creativity and imagination. They come up with new ways in which the Gospel and culture can interact. They dream dreams and put these dreams into action- they are dreamers who do, and find gazebos! Pathfinders will often find opposition from those who do not share their vision and who prefer the outmoded ways of doing things. Pathfinders will not settle for the mediocre. They are radicals.

Pathfinding dissenters are innovative, prophetic and responsible. They advocate risk-taking and recognise their role in the evangelisation of culture. They are not 'adaptors', who maintain the new within traditional structures. They are innovators, who are community-minded not individualistic. They are compass followers!

Dissenters expand horizons and are 'upside-down' thinkers. The story of the rich young ruler (Mark 10:17-22) is an example of how Jesus dissented from the established norm and promoted such thinking. This story illustrates how sometimes we have to give up everything, to throw in our lot and commit ourselves to the cause.

1

This will allow us to see God beyond the sacred spaces and be able to make connections in our everyday lives. By seeing God only in church on a Sunday, at home groups, or in whatever other contexts we deem to be 'spiritual' spaces, we separate the secular and the sacred. We need to open up the possibilities to allow God to permeate the whole of our lives. The rich young ruler had fooled himself into thinking he was open and faithful, when in reality he wasn't. If we close ourselves off to new possibilities, we risk being similarly fooled and closed off to what God might be asking of us.

Pete Rollins illustrates this further when he talks about the comic hero Batman.[10] He argues that if Bruce Wayne (Batman) channelled his money into education, then Gotham wouldn't actually have need of Batman.

Equally, we would ask if it is acceptable to develop a creative worship space in a church building where God is confined, or whether we can risk changing the way we approach G-d so we might discover the un-sanitised, scandalous creator who resisted being put in a temple building in the first place?

Community is important. It is vital for us to not only be part of the local geographical community, but to work with the community in unity. This immersion is a bit like childbirth: painful, messy, energy-sapping, a hard slog, awe-inspiring, emotional and life-giving. It is agony and ecstasy. It is only by committing ourselves fully to following G-d to new and unexpected places that we will truly see transformative change happen.

You may feel a sense of trepidation and exhilaration, so as we ready ourselves for the journey we try to familiarise ourselves with these new tools and try them out. There may not be a manual telling us how and when to use them but we can consider how best they might be used. But there is still more to learn before we commence our journey....

Symbiosis in Practice

As pathfinding dissenters, we have learnt that the less you embrace dualism (in our case, this means separating our beliefs from our actions, the sacred from the secular and our church-lives from the rest of our lives) the more you will see God in the context you are working in and discover ways to connect with what He is doing. This in itself becomes part of the journey that enables pathfinding dissenters to be the innovative, prophetic people they are called to be.

Culture clash

Our experiences of being young people might be very different to the youth culture we observe today. For example, in the 1990s, if you wanted to meet up with your friends at Greenbelt (a Christian Music and Arts Festival), you had to leave a note fixed to a notice board on site. If you were lucky, your friend might locate the message amongst the hundreds of other notes jumbled on the board and meet you at the relevant spot. Where once we communicated face-to-face and by telephone (and with good old paper and pen), we now communicate by text, Facebook, tweeting and instant messaging. Today, young people grow up in an instant culture where you can do most things from the comfort of your own sofa – even buying or downloading this book! It is no wonder that we sometimes find ourselves feeling like aliens in a strange land when encountering today's youth culture. In this respect, the needle of our compass swings significantly towards *Culture*.

Having briefly explored the valley of post-Christendom, we now venture forth into the jungle of post-modernism, a broad term that describes the cultural environment we currently find ourselves in. Post-modernity will be a familiar term to most and it is certainly one people use a lot. We can see the influences of this cultural movement on post-Christendom and how a post-modern culture has shaped western society. Some of this shift into post-modernity can be seen through the disengagement with traditional religious and cultural beliefs. Today's culture is influenced by many idealisms, voices and beliefs that might have been suppressed in the 'modern' world where people tended to adhere more to traditional worldviews.

It's a bit like television. Previously we had three television channels. Fast-forward a few decades and now there are hundreds! The influence of the few has been diluted by a plethora of choice. Not only that, but we have gone 'global'. The influence of globalization can be seen everywhere from the food we eat, to the clothes we wear, the music we listen to and the films we choose to watch. Not only is this instant culture influenced by what is happening here in the UK, but also by global cultural and faith dynamics.

Where once a set of traditional social norms dictated cultural 'modern thought', now there are a multitude of influences from which we can pick and choose. Some suggest the post-modern world

1

is more superficial. Even the term post-modern is an anathema: how can you be 'after' or 'post' the new or modern thing? The post-modern context is one in which we are bombarded with images and information in a fast-paced, ever-changing world. The pick-and-mix culture of post-modernity allows us to choose what we want from wherever we want, when we want.

However, we are currently seeing a further shift, with people nostalgically adopting traditions of the past: cooking things from scratch, 'make do and mend', vintage clothing and growing our own food have once again become popular. Taking things from a previous era and remaking them, along with re-inventing them anew has also gained in popularity. This, coupled with the ever increasing pace of developing technologies and interconnectedness through social media, has led some to conclude that we are in a period of super or hyper-modernity – an age where everything is part of a large melting pot. All of life, religion, culture, science, business and consumption can be refashioned, remodelled and remoulded for today's society. For example, take the radio. You buy one with retro credentials and it wouldn't look out of place in a 1950s kitchen; the only difference is it is digital. It is a reimagining of the old, borrowing from a previous era to make something new and contemporary, fitting today's world.

This shift in cultural thought may also impact the debate around young people and spirituality. Some say that there is a lack of spiritual curiosity amongst young people. This view would fit in with the frippery of the post-modern. Yet our work with young people suggests this isn't the case. There may not be the same sort of open or connected spirituality that we would have recognised in the past,[i] but perhaps there is something buried[ii] which is more easily uncovered within the context of a mutual relationship. This can be seen in the discussion described earlier where the young people were talking about going on a pilgrimage. Perhaps it is a rejection by young people of the language used and the approaches undertaken rather than a rejection of spirituality itself. As well as seeing Flow as an example, we will discuss shortly where this 'buried spirituality' is being fostered and uncovered with young people through, for example, dance, football and conversations. Whether you are working with churched or non-churched young people, the same is true: church, with its 'Christendom' mind-set, seems more and more at odds with the post-modern and post-Christendom worldviews.

---

[i] For a further discussion about this, see Collins-Mayo, Mayo and Nash (2010).

[ii] For a further discussion about this, see Rankin (2005).

In Acts 17 we read that Paul, when in Athens, noticed the people had an altar to the 'unknown God' (verse 23). Paul spoke to the people of Athens in a way they could understand. He highlighted their recognition of the unknown God and offered to tell them about Him. In the hyper-modern, post-Christian world, there is a need to move beyond just repackaging the message, to engaging in a 'reciprocal' or mutual journeying between Christianity and culture. As discussed previously there is a need to embrace all the points of the compass (*Bible*, *Tradition* and *Culture*) and hold each in tension with the others. All are equally valuable within the new landscape.

Sharing in young people's culture

Inculturation (in this context) is a theological term used to describe presenting Christianity to a non-Christian culture in such a way that a church can organically develop out of that culture whilst being influenced by the culture. It is the intertwined relationship between the new culture and the Christian culture that should shape how we do church and mission. In our case, the people inhabiting the Land of Dragons are young people and so it is their youth culture that has something to offer.

By engaging with the culture, you allow the reciprocal process of inculturation to happen. In order for it to develop, you might have to step back and allow this new thing to evolve on its own terms – even if you do not know where it will lead or what it will look like. There is mutuality about the relationship as, not only does the culture change and evolve, it also changes the way in which Christianity is expressed through the inculturation process. In this way we see ourselves become inculturators: curators of the new ways rather than leaders who shape it. This reinforces the idea that our role is as mediators.

> *The young people were keen to start redeveloping the skate park. The plan was to raise the necessary finances to extend and light the existing park. In order to get the ball rolling, the young people wanted to host a skate and bike event. On hearing that a local project had mobile ramps, they decided a visit to see them was in order. It was great to arrive at the youth centre and see the hall transformed into an indoor skate park and the accompanying graffiti project that was happening outside. The young people quickly made themselves at home, using the ramps, testing them out and thinking about possible layouts if we used the same set up back in Chard. Halfway through the evening, they were surprised to be asked to stop*

1

skating and listen to a short talk but, being in a minority, sat down with the rest of the group. As we got in the car to return home, their shock and surprise at being made to listen to a Christian talk was evident. They couldn't understand how the group simply accepted this from the leaders. I explained that the youth workers there had a good relationship and friendship with the young people and so this was something that they had worked towards over time. In the same way that we could talk about Flow, because they knew us and wanted to explore more, their workers could chat to the local young people in this different style. They pointed out the difference between conversation and dialogue around Flow with being made to sit and listen, but they were happy to accept that different projects worked in different ways.

Richard Passmore

The notion of having a 'God Spot' perhaps typifies a Christendom approach, as those delivering it assume a position of power and force others to listen to it. Even though this God Spot used a creative and interactive approach and was delivered by very skilled workers, the young people we worked with perceived this as something 'different' to what they were familiar with. The difference was that we were working with the young people in a more 'inculturalised' way, which is why they picked up on the difference between a two-way mutual dialogical approach and an upfront delivery. I know the workers of the project did not intend to speak dogmatically, but the approach they adopted meant that, even though the story was creative and well delivered with appropriate language, it fell short for our group. The core reason was that it was told from outside of the context of a relationship between the worker and our group. Secondly, this was compounded by our group's lack of confidence to develop a more dialogical approach – which was essentially down to the power dynamics of having a person delivering a talk. This brings us back to our compass: here the needle might have got stuck between *Tradition* and the Bible, when it actually needed to be held in tension within the three elements of *Bible*, *Culture* and *Tradition* to make it more relevant and empowering. It also demonstrates the difference between what we would advocate, the inculturalisation process (a transforming approach), rather than enculturalisation (the conditioning or socialisation of people).

Symbiosis in Practice

The medium is the message. No matter how slick, how creative or how inspired you feel about the way you 'communicate' with the young people you work with, if it is not in the right medium, it risks having little or no impact. We should engage with young people where they are and on their terms. Don't be afraid to go out on a limb, but remember that perhaps just having a conversation with a few young people will have more impact than you sitting them down and talking at them about Jesus. The key to all of this, of course, is relationship. Without relationship, you don't have trust. Without trust, you have little to build with. Trust takes time; you need to work at it. If you get to know the young people, then the way to talk to them about God and spirituality is something that will grow organically.

In recent times, the public has fallen out with the UK banking industry. We have seen protests across the country, most notably those led by the Occupy Movement. There seems to be a general mistrust of many traditional institutions: political parties, government and big business to name but a few. Some people feel the same way about the institution of 'church' and religion, cultivating a level of distrust, apathy, and unwillingness to commit to it. Increasingly the church is being viewed as just a building and not a body of people.

The story above about the 'God Spot' illustrates that evangelistic models that used to work might be irrelevant to today's society. Therefore, we need to explore new ways of telling the stories and creating a dialogical approach where the story can be engaged with and reinterpreted mutually with the group. In a culture where truth is relative, the classical ideas of evangelism, of 'preaching' the gospel, appear to hold less currency with people than they might once have done. This is not to say that the cultural landscape is devoid of resources for mission, but like any explorer we need to discover the resources that are inherent within the post-modern condition and reshape these as tools for the journey. Our compass needle now points us more in the direction of the *Bible*.

An example of what can happen when you do adopt a more dialogical approach occurred when we explored with a group of young people the Parable of the Wedding Banquet as told in Matthew 22:1-14.

1

'*Reading from below*' is a liberation theology approach to exploring the Bible in community. The approach involves trying to read the text from the position of someone on the outside, someone poor or powerless. When we explored the passage with the young people reading it in this way, they interpreted it quite differently from how it is usually perceived (where God is seen as the king).

If we have a view of God as being with, alongside or among the poor and marginalised, in this story He is in the highways and byways. Using this as the start point made it impossible for the young people to see the king as God or the son as Jesus. This led to an interpretation of the parable as a critique of organised religion or power.

In the young people's eyes, they saw a king keen to make alliances with the rich farmers and business people who invited these wealthy people to his party in order to impress them. These business people are obviously powerful as, not only do they have the opportunity and means to kill the servants the king first sent to them, but subsequently the passage states that the king needs to subdue them by the use of force with armies – not just a couple of henchmen.

Then, in order to not be seen as a loser, the king needs to have some people come to the party so he invites (coerces?) poorer people to attend. Tradition at the time dictated that the groom's father provided the right clothes for the wedding party guests. One person refuses to wear the clothes provided by the manipulative, politically savvy, violent and coercive monarch. This one person refuses to play the game by the rules of the powerful and is cast out into the darkness with the outcasts.

This is where the young people saw Jesus in the story – someone not willing to go along with the power plays of the day; someone who stands up for justice; someone who reads the motives of the powerful; someone who stands outside of those systems. The Kingdom of heaven is about putting other people first, standing up for righteousness, speaking out for the voiceless and living in a way that is radically different to the established ways of the world. We think the young people are onto something! We have produced a version of this story that may resonate more with the sentiments behind the aforementioned Occupy Movement:

> *Making money had not been difficult for Jimmy. He had a good*
> *stack of cash from his dad, invested it in property, employed*
> *builders, did up houses and soon started to diversify. At first*
> *he bought the building supplies yard – that way not only could*

he control the builders but also the prices. After having some stuff nicked, he started a private security business that was soon being used by most of the local shops.

Then he diversified into rentals: buying land and building small properties for renters that couldn't afford much. This wasn't generosity. It was an economy of scale. Lots of small flats brought in the same rent as a large house.

In an age of no welfare state or government hand-outs, he pretty much controlled the town, owned most of the land and was Mayor in all but name. He had a close network of business associates who he thought of as friends, but they knew who was really in charge. As he and a few others grew richer, the town grew poorer, so Jimmy extended his security business as a sort of local police force to keep the locals in line. This meant he could increase his charges to other businesses to keep them safe and everyone knows 'it takes money to make money'.

Jimmy considered himself happily married, with a mistress or two on the side, and two children (that he knew of). When his daughter turned twenty-one, it was time to celebrate with a masked ball. The theme was 'winter' and everyone would be provided with appropriate clothes, to ensure the elegance of the event and that the theme was suitably expressed.

After many months of planning, he sent out invites to the great and good of the community – the people Jimmy thought of as friends. A few simply didn't reply, probably because Jimmy's private police force had been too heavy-handed recently and the taxes felt more like extortion money. A few replied and said they were too busy to attend, not really wanting to come but trying to keep Jimmy on side. As the day drew near, the marquee for the party was put up on the local football pitch. Two others were erected as changing rooms for guests. Caterers were bought in, musicians prepped and waiters found. The only hitch was that no one was coming. Jimmy grew impatient and arranged a second invite as it made good business sense – a good party was a chance to network and make a few more contacts.

Word had spread amongst the business leaders that no one was attending the party. They became bolder about their excuses or non-replies – in collective solidarity they felt more secure about saying 'no' to Jimmy. But their 'security' was short lived. In a rage Jimmy ordered his security people to

1

break their windows. When the owners went for replacements he hiked the prices of repairs and controlled the supply of new glass! He increased the rent of these 'friends', and ordered the actual Mayor to evict those who didn't replace the damaged windows, on the grounds it 'wasn't in keeping' and degraded the neighbourhood. Soon Jimmy had driven away, beaten up, or simply killed his supposed friends and business allies.

Not wanting the party to fail, he invited the tenants from the flats. He knew these people would scrub up well enough and he had the right clothes ready for them to wear. He would need to replace the business leaders he had driven out anyway and might recruit suitable people at the event. The invitation was delivered by the private police force and it was made clear attendance was non-negotiable. Besides, rumours and stories of what had happened to the great and good of the town were rife.

As one of the tenants explained to her husband, they had to go. Even the people who had a bit of money behind them and had refused Jimmy's invitation had been attacked – 'who were they to refuse?' Besides, there may be a future in it and at least she got to wear a fine dress and eat well at Jimmy's expense.

The party started, and was going with a swing. Contacts were being made as Jimmy identified a few people to rent the shops and agreed to replace a few windows at cost price to get things moving again. The only blot had been the appearance of a small tent occupying the mouth of the goal on the football pitch. No one pointed it out to Jimmy and besides, what did it matter? But Jimmy had noticed it, and started to make plans to get it removed the following day. He would do it legally and without fuss. Tonight he would focus on the party – after all, life goes on.

It was later that evening that Jimmy spotted him – well he could hardly be missed in his ripped jeans and t-shirt that simply said 'Occupy'. Everyone else had worn the clothes provided as instructed. "The audacity! The sheer nerve!", Jimmy thought, to come in here, eat the food, drink the wine, and not wear the right clothes. But by wearing a simple t-shirt the occupier showed the fine dresses and suits for what they were – a charade, a falsehood to open doors and enable the mistakes of the past to be repeated. Jimmy saw the irony, the threat, and how powerful the powerless man in the t-shirt was.

He called security, had the man stripped naked, beaten, and killed.

The lack of resistance from the man was breath-taking; his quiet humility seemed to pave a way for all the onlookers to take a different path if they too would lose the trappings of power. But for many the cost would be too high a price to pay.

1

Chapter 3 – Collapsing the Bridge

'How do we encourage young people into church?' A familiar mission model is that of the bridge – where there is a gap between life inside church and life outside church and the youth group, event or initiative is seen as the bridge young people cross to make the transition from outside to inside. To reduce relational youth work to nothing more than a tool to get young people into church is to miss the heartbeat of the incarnation. The bridge model is poor missiology and weak ecclesiology. It is not ill-intentioned and it is utilised by well-meaning people who want to engage in mission. The problem is it often just doesn't cut it anymore: it is an outdated view of mission. The leap from youth group to church is so huge that not many make it. Of those few that do, many subsequently fall away. This is evident in the decreasing number of young people attending church, the increasing body of research about what encompasses effective youth ministry and the ever-increasing average age of church congregations. At the very core of our methods and stance is 'collapsing' the bridge idea and reimagining how church can be grown from scratch in today's society.[i]

Ephesians 5:32 describes the relationship between Christ and the church as 'a profound mystery'. This is difficult for us to comprehend when what we really want to do is to define what it is, pin it down and give it form. As we discussed in Chapter 2, our western approach to truth can cause us to struggle with the concept of mystery as our default positioning might be a desire to pigeonhole what church is and does.

We also need to read this passage from Ephesians within a broader context. We should note that Christ gave Himself up for the church to make her holy and blameless. I am sure there are some things we, as individuals and leaders, may need to give up in order to liberate the church so that she may become all that she might. In order for this to happen we need to put aside any notion of 'power'. Christ became powerless on the cross, which opened the way to truth and reconciliation. If Christ could do this, how much more so should we, the church, put aside our power in order to liberate others so that they can be enlightened and reconciled to God?

This means acknowledging that we do not know what 'church' might look like as a result of our work with young people. We need to have no preconceived ideas of how church might develop in the new Land

---

[i] In *Off the Beaten Track*, Richard also argues that the idea of mission as a bridge into church holds little weight Biblically and is not consistent with the images of church offered in scripture.

of Dragons. This doesn't mean we should not venture forth together into the new land intending to begin the journey towards being church/community, but that what emerges might not look like what we thought it might look like.

To think outside of the box of what we call 'church' can be frightening, challenging and cause uncertainty. But we are inviting you on the most thrilling, life-changing, dangerous journey – one where not only do you lead but are also led; where you will learn as well as teach; where we can journey with one another and, out of this reciprocal relationship, all participate in discovering a new way. This immersion with others, this mutual inclusivity, is at the core of what we believe creates space for new ways of being church and for finding enlightenment in the most unexpected places.

As previously mentioned, those of us in the Chard project decided to embark on a pilgrimage together with some of the young people we were working with. So a group of eleven young people, two leaders and their families made their way to Cornwall. The group would not only go on day trips to various skate parks in the area, but also spend time with the leaders and their families. During this time we told another story about Flow.

Abs and Flow

In a town not so far from here, there was man known as Abs. The town was a pretty desolate place with not much going on, so Abs grew up learning how to skate and ride. As soon as he put his foot on his first board he knew he was born to ride. As he rode he experienced life and energy in a way he had never known before. The more he rode the more he flowed with this life and energy.

Slowly Abs began to understand that the life and energy was beyond him – it was not created by him, or generated by him – but as he forgot himself in the ride he would experience it more and more. Abs began to call this life and energy 'Flow'. He started to recognise when Flow was, and was not, present. The more he understood and experienced Flow, the more he wanted to be in Flow all the time. Slowly Abs felt Flow beginning to communicate with him: it was strange, unnerving, and Abs was not sure at first if he was imagining things. But he knew Flow. Unsure, he murmured – to himself as much as to the Flow – that he wanted to experience Flow all the time.

Whether it was a voice, an internal impression of a voice, or just something in his mind Abs was unsure, but he knew it was Flow. But what Flow was communicating to him seemed a strange contradiction. He felt the voice was telling him that if he really wanted to know Flow then he would have to break his skateboard. Abs was confused. Wasn't it through riding that he first really began to experience Flow? Wasn't it through those moments of laughter and relief after pulling the best hand plant, or kick flip that Flow was most present? Yet Abs longed for more and had grown to trust Flow and so reluctantly he made his way to the skate park quarter, the highest ramp around, to smash his board on the edge of the concrete ramp.

Vincent Donovan, a Catholic missionary to the Masai, speaks of how he found ways of engaging with the East African culture by making the gospel relevant and meaningful to them.[11] Donovan stressed that salvation is accessible through the local culture, customs and traditions.

Donovan went to the Masai tribes and told them the story of Abraham – a story he thought would resonate with them as a semi-nomadic people. This is what we tried to do with the young people we worked with. We took a familiar Bible story and re-contextualised it to be understood by a different culture. Using familiar language that was relevant to the young people enabled us to share with them the story of Abraham and Isaac (Genesis 22:1-12).

Following the telling of the story (after which no interpretation was given) we chatted about it and questions were asked. One young man was particularly anxious about trying to work it out, asking all sorts of questions and trying to get a handle on what the story meant. He did not see how you could break your board and Flow all the time, or even experience Flow when not riding.

The following day we went to this very impressive skate park, but it was too wet to ride. This same young man stood at the bottom of the skate park's bowl (a large bowl shaped 'ramp') and shouted up, "Hey Rich, I think I know what Abs was on about now. I can feel Flow even though I'm not riding".

Paul Minear suggests there are ninety-six metaphors in the Bible for church and all carry a sense of being and doing, or going.[12] By engaging in mission intentionally, to be and grow church, we begin to align ourselves with this sense of being and doing, together feeling our way into a new way of church/community. The collapsed bridge between mission and church challenges the idea of church planting as we cannot gain a fixed idea of what church is from the

Biblical narrative, and we cannot know from outside of a context what sort of church is relevant for that community. A new church needs to emerge and grow, to be nurtured rather than to be forced in the particular direction that we want it to go in – however well-meaning this intention is.

If the bridge is collapsed, how do we understand mission and move forward? We must find a new metaphor, one more fitting to the 'mystery'. We think the metaphor of 'tacking' helpfully portrays what needs to happen. When a boat or ship is sailing from A to B, it cannot sail directly into the wind – it would just be blown backwards! As it cannot sail in a direct straight line, it has to 'tack', or zigzag, in order to progress from one point to another and to catch the wind in its sails. This notion of tacking is an approach to mission inspired by the life of Jesus – he had no direct route, no plan of action, and whenever he had an encounter on the journey, there were important transformations.

In order to be and grow church we need to see church as both the journey we are on and the destination we are heading to. This is the *being* and *doing* which Minear highlights.

On this particular journey though, it's not just about the 'boat'. The boat cannot dictate the direction of travel; the direction is influenced by the wind, the waves, the shoreline, the current and the depth of the waters. There is a bigger picture and influence in which we have to immerse ourselves. It is not just about our vision, but about allowing the greater 'vision' to be shaped by those around us as we connect and have relationship with them. They help to guide the way, to show the new direction.

Engaging in mission intentionally, both being an expression of and growing church, creates change. It reframes the question from 'when does this become church?' (which limits what might subsequently take place) and instead starts with the question 'what is God doing?'. This question embraces endless possibilities. The approach to youth work we are advocating then becomes a way of being that has a missional spirituality that moves us beyond the dualistic false divisions that have tended to haunt the church thus far in its history.

So we are going on a journey. We don't know what the landscape will look like, but we have some useful tools for the job. We are inculturators, ready to engage with the culture of the young people we encounter. By engaging with young people, we will also be enlightened and have a broader view and understanding of God, a

1

growing recognition that the god we know may not be G-d. As Mister Eckhart prayed "God rid me of god".[13] This further goes to support the reciprocal nature of mission. When you embark on a journey with the intention of being and growing church, it is a journey that fuels your understanding of God, enabling you to see the missionary endeavour as an act of worship to God, encountering the presence of G-d throughout the whole process. This in turn brings us full circle to an understanding, not of mission as a bridge into church, but of church as a dynamic, subversive interaction between the individual, community and the missio Dei on a redemptive path together.

We also do not journey alone. We are joined by others who will influence and experiment with us. This journey on which we are to embark has no mapped-out route. Everyone has as much influence on the turns we take as ourselves. We watch, learn, engage with and participate as a group of people committed to the journey. We are in the Land of Dragons – the unchartered territories. We are growing church as a verb not a noun: an active, emerging, living, breathing and organic movement not just a static, bound or restricted name we give to a building or to something we do on a Sunday. We encourage you to take the first step in to the most thrilling adventure of your lives. So take a deep breath, strap on your walking shoes, allow the sun to warm your face and take the first step onto pathways new.

Chapter 4 – Unfolding Symbiotic Youth Work

In this chapter we describe more fully what we mean by Symbiotic Youth Work.

Some of the young people we work with are helping run an event called *Rampfest* in a neighbouring town. They have been talking about how this is the first time the towns in the area have come together and about the importance of breaking down the history of antipathy between the young people from the various towns. These young volunteers are also keen to start a StreetSpace project in a new area themselves. In response to a text thanking him for attending the team meeting, one of the young volunteers texted back:

> *No thank you! It's us three who should be thanking you and the others for giving us the opportunity in which we can see things from a different perspective and change our roles, to help us become what I feel are better people. The experience has been brilliant and I'm looking forward to becoming more involved, helping and potentially changing the lives of young people. Top youth leader I am HAhaHA.*

As we have seen in previous chapters, we have started to see a pattern of working with young people that relies on relationship, reciprocation, the mutuality between church and mission, process and outcome, young person and youth worker. The story above shows how this approach unfolds a new way of being for the young person and indicates someone well on their way to becoming fully human.

For some time we have been thinking that we need a new term to describe what a particular set of Christian practitioners previously called 'relational youth work'. The term 'relational youth work' began to be used by a group of practitioners largely working with young people on the edge of society. It grew to become a way of engaging more generally with those outside of church as we know it. Now we find that it is an anathema to not see youth work as relational. If it is to be called youth work then we believe it has to be relational. We as Christians seek to be incarnational – just as Jesus was God incarnate to the world, so must we be – but this language hangs heavy with Christian dogma. Historically, for us as youth workers, the term 'relational youth work' has had a more profound meaning than just that of being in relationship with the young people. It encapsulates an ideology that embodies Christ's example of loving, caring, nurturing, teaching and challenging. It is through this 'relational'

1

aspect of youth work and following the missio Dei that we are enriched and purposeful in our endeavours. Relational youth work came to be a way of life as we recognised that our salvation was inextricably linked to the emancipation of the young people we serve.

As the strands have converged, the context has become more post-Christian and the language of church is shifting. Some of the informing values of relational youth work have evolved and some have been lost. The term 'incarnational youth work', is often used to try to express something beyond simple contextualisation. This term encompasses something that cannot be simply articulated and embraces ideas about: a person's wholeness being wrapped up in the shalom of the community; an on-going journey; the restoring of creation and a sense of powerlessness – values and dynamics we need to be reminded of (and which we explore further in Chapter 6) if we are going to see the Kingdom continue to emerge. However this term is particularly Christian and potentially dualistic, which is something we are keen to avoid for reasons already discussed (see Chapter 2 – Unpacking the Landscape).

We prefer the notion of reciprocal approaches to youth work and mission – the idea that together we see something new emerge. This leaves a conundrum of which term to use to describe such work. 'Reciprocal youth work' and 'emerging youth work' are both viable options. Probably the term that best encompasses what we are trying to express (but might mean the least to those unfamiliar with the term) is 'sobornostic youth work', where we journey with young people towards wholeness for all of society, creation, ourselves and others in order to unfold a new way of living and being. We will discuss what we mean by 'sobornostic' later in this chapter, but for now will define it as a spiritual and communal unity that arises as people set aside individual quests in order to develop like-minded interests. It is a word that sums up an important part of our journey and one that helped lead us to a term that is hopefully more easily understood by both Christian and secular practitioners: 'Symbiotic Youth Work'.[i]

By using this term 'Symbiotic Youth Work' we are seeking to illustrate that it is not just the worker who has something to impart

---

[i] Richard was involved in discussion with other youth practitioners – Richard Davies and Nick Shepherd – regarding the *character* of work undertaken (e.g. youth work, youth ministry) and the *mode* or *approach* to this (e.g. relational, incarnational). What has come out in the unfolding discussion is that the two (character and mode) are two sides of the same coin. This is discussed further in Section Two as we see the interconnectedness of values-led practice and the genetics of symbiotic youth work.

to the young people they work with, but that the young people can also teach the worker. We work it out by working together; there is no pre-determined curriculum and set of activities! This approach allows us as youth workers to set aside inflexible programmes, fixed outcome goals and ticking boxes to meet targets, allowing space for us to pursue the missio Dei, wherever that may lead.

So what is symbiosis? Symbiosis is a biological term describing two organisms that live in close association with each other, to protect or ensure their survival. There are three types of symbiosis. The first is *commensalism*: where the association benefits one organism, but does nothing for the other. The second is *parasitism*: which benefits one and harms the other. The aspect of symbiosis, which applies in our youth work context, is the third category, that of *mutuality* or *mutualism*: where the relationship is beneficial to both organisms. This symbiotic process of mutualism is defined as:

> "The relationship between two different species of organisms that are interdependent; each gains and benefits from the other. A relationship between different species where both of the organisms in question benefit from the presence of the other."[14]

An important aspect of symbiosis is that it is formed in nature: 'He said to them "...Go into all the world and preach the gospel to all creation"' (Mark 16:15). There are many examples of symbiotic relationships; like that of the Acacia tree and the Pseudomyrmex ants. The tree offers the ants food and a place to nest. In return the ants protect the tree from other insects (and the occasional giraffe!) that would cause the tree damage. To adopt symbiosis is to take a move away from the individualism that is so prevalent in western society, even within Christian culture where we often talk about our personal experiences of salvation, God, journeying, prayer and worship. It is a move from individuality into community. Every piece of youth work is different, so allow the process of your engagement in Symbiotic Youth Work to develop and evolve organically. Forget religion, work on relationships and don't be afraid of failure!

Youth culture is always shifting, moving and changing. What you encountered five years ago might not be what you encounter today. Engaging in a symbiotic relationship with the young people you work with means that, in most basic of terms, you adapt or die. The youth work we are engaged in will always be changing – we need to change with it. By youth worker and young people mutually engaging with one another as person and person, this process naturally evolves and makes it naturally contextual. The youth

1

worker does not take power or dictate the nature and content of the work. It is the dynamics of this evolving symbiotic relationship that shape the work we do with young people, and determines where the power resides. There is a freedom in approaching our work with no pre-determined agenda[i] and without fixed outcomes. However, it is also daunting, seeming to fly in the face of conventional approaches and the increasing move towards more institutionalised practices and outcomes-driven approaches. It is a risk, but a calculated one. We engage in this type of youth work with the knowledge that, through the implementation of good youth work practices and policies as our safety net (not only for ourselves but also the young people we serve), we can journey to a new place together.

Animation and sketching out the future

Dan Stiver, [15] identifies three strands that typify post-modernity that help us with the symbiotic reimagining of church in this new context. Firstly, post-modernity is a critique of the modern, a kind of anti-modern reaction. Without modernity we would not have post-modernity. Secondly, it is a paradigm shift or a change of worldview; we are in transition. Thirdly and most importantly, it is a 'sketch of the future'.

If we accept that culture can teach us something new regarding church, then this concept of a 'sketch of the future' could enable us to re-imagine the church in a new and radical way, and co-operatively produce this with the culture we are in. Part of this is being able to 'read' and set the pace for this relationship – it is not about dictating the relationship in a particular direction, but about using the tools that you have to support a mutually-beneficial organic development. Let's look at the concept of socio-cultural animation, which explores how we interact and participate with a community of young people. Using informal education and community learning, the 'animator' animates – giving life to the inanimate. The animator is engaging with the young people to enable them to develop, participate and liberate themselves and us. For example, a local project was heavily involved in bush craft activities with young people; there was something intrinsically spiritual for them being outside in nature. The worker animated this by proposing that one Sunday they explored together ways they

---

[i] For example, if there is a pre-determined agenda to stop the young people from underage drinking, the work you engage in, the conversations you have and the activities you might put on will all be influenced by this agenda. By having no pre-determined agenda, but by working intentionally (discussed more in Values-Led Practice, Chapter 6) you allow a more equal power balance between worker and young people.

could use the bush craft experiences they had gained to connect with the power behind the nature – using the word 'church' was helpful in connecting the cultural bush craft experience to the Christian tradition. The activities developed were simple, such as writing on leaves and burning them, but the simplicity itself was powerful. This notion of 'pacing' or animation will be discussed in more depth at the end of this chapter.

Mission and hospitality

Mission is not primarily an activity of the church, but an attribute of God. God is a missionary God. It is not the church that has a mission of salvation to fulfil in the world; it is the mission of the Son and the Spirit through the Father in which the church is included. There is church because there is mission, not vice versa.[16]

Firstly, we need to understand what mission is, not what it may have become. Mission is not a project of the church, it isn't something we do in addition to church; rather it is the DNA of Christianity. We have already discussed in Chapter 3 that church and mission are symbiotically connected through mystery and the exploration of metaphor. We also see in John 1 that God is a missionary God who crosses frontiers. In the Bible we see the Father sends the Son (1 John 4:9), the Father and Son send the Spirit (John 14:26), and together they send the church (Matthew 28:16-20). In *Transforming Mission* David Bosch highlights that community is the "primary bearer of mission"[17] and, as we see demonstrated in the gospels, community was often the context for Jesus' ministry. Whilst Jesus was itinerant and was not rooted in a single geographical community, he travelled with the disciples as a form of community and mainly spoke to groups or in family settings. His ministry was people-centred, with groups and community being a core aspect of this. Bosch further highlights that the relationship between mission and church must be more closely considered and one in which all are "directly involved".[18]

Jesus' ministry evidenced the importance of community and inclusion. He demonstrated a new way of being an inclusive community with the disciples, the women, and others excluded from society that was way beyond anything ever seen before (for example: Luke 19:1-10, Zacchaeus; Matthew 19:14, the little children; and Luke 7:36-50, the sinful woman). At times these communities were temporary and show Jesus ministering in a community context – the temporary nature does not undermine that implicit value of community. (See later in Chapter 5 about the role of

Temporary Autonomous Zones or T.A.Z.)

Several of these Bible passages see Jesus using symbiosis as a means to foster community. For example, the disciples may have struggled with Zaccheus because he was a tax collector. By going to Zaccheus' house, Jesus demonstrated his acceptance of him, allowing a new form of inclusive community to unfold. We see symbiosis in action where all those were involved in the encounter may have been changed: Zaccheus, his family, his community, the community of disciples and even possibly Jesus. Christ's new covenant is one of people – not only the remnant of Israel but also of those on the outside, far beyond these boundaries. So we intentionally and symbiotically set out to be and grow church, recognising we are mutually held together with God, the community and young people.

Symbiotic Youth Work requires openness and hospitality. Hospitality is a word often used today to describe what some missional communities are getting involved in with their friends, neighbours and local communities. Often this means a group of Christians getting together, hosting their neighbours who are non-churched, and sharing a meal with them. For us, in the work we do with the people we encounter, hospitality takes on a mutual meaning that moves beyond entertaining others (which it can sometimes become) towards creating a shared and received space. We have also been inspired by Jesus' own approach to mission in the sending out of the seventy-two.

> After this the Lord appointed seventy-two others and sent them two by two ahead of him to every town and place where he was about to go. He told them, "The harvest is plentiful, but the workers are few. Ask the Lord of the harvest, therefore, to send out workers into his harvest field. Go! I am sending you out like lambs among wolves. Do not take a purse or bag or sandals; and do not greet anyone on the road.
>
> When you enter a house, first say, 'Peace to this house.' If a man of peace is there, your peace will rest on him; if not, it will return to you. Stay in that house, eating and drinking whatever they give you, for the worker deserves his wages. Do not move around from house to house. When you enter a town and are welcomed, eat what is set before you. Heal the sick who are there and tell them 'The Kingdom of God is near you.' But when you enter a town and are not welcomed go into its streets and say, 'Even the dust of your town that sticks to our feet we wipe off against you. Yet be sure of this: The kingdom

*of God is near'. I tell you, it will be more bearable on that day
for Sodom than for that town."*
Luke 10:1-12

There are many challenges in this passage, and many instructions.
Firstly Jesus sent them out; not as individuals, but in pairs. He said
to them that the "harvest is plentiful, but the workers are few". In
our work on the edges of society, we can often feel isolated and
alone, but we go with God's blessing. You take nothing with you for
the journey; no purse, bag or sandals, you are reliant on the
hospitality of others. You do not anticipate what the journey will
require or what things you might need to take with you. You leave it
all behind. In so doing you make yourselves vulnerable, both to God
and to the community you are serving. It is not a place of comfort,
but a place of discomfort.

Jesus does not promise that everything will be easy. "Go! I am
sending you out like lambs among wolves" is not the most
motivational of speeches! Hospitality is also turned on its head – the
disciples would not be hosting the meal but would have to be invited
to "stay in that house, eating and drinking whatever they give you".
This is not something that they should humbly accept but expect, for
"the worker deserves his wages". It is important to balance the need
for consistency with young people, i.e. that God may call us to stay
in one place, and the idea that we are a pilgrim people moving on
with God. A member of the StreetSpace team said recently that one
of the most important lessons to learn is that of 'stickability'. There
is a great reward for sticking around. It is often how relationships
form and how needs are met. In this passage we see Jesus telling
the disciples to go on a journey (to the Land of Dragons), but once
they find a welcome, they should pause and stay in that place for a
while: being with the community, serving, loving and helping heal
them; that they should stick around until it is time to move on in
search of more dragons.

We believe God is already present in the Land of Dragons as there is
no place on earth without God. Our role is to get in on the act and
walk with God and the young people on the prepared path to this
place; just as Jesus did when he saw what his Father in heaven was
doing (John 5:19) and just as the seventy-two were encouraged by
Jesus to do what they had seen him doing. Following the missio Dei
is about process and outcome: actions need to match words. There
is a need for liberation to recognise all that we can be with God.

1

Symbiosis in Practice

Get involved. The disciples didn't know where they were going and did not do much preparation for the journey. They just went, lived amongst the people and were community with them, working alongside them and sharing stories.

Church and mission: two-sides of the same coin?

When we begin to re-look at church and mission in this symbiotic way, we see that they are two sides of the same coin and not separate entities. Following the missio Dei in this post-Christendom era is as much about doing mission as it is about being church. Returning to the Biblical images of attitude and action, you could argue that what most people know as church is about the attitude/being, and mission is the course of action. This is slightly over-simplified, as we must hold in tension the possibility that an attitude can be mission-orientated. Adopting a both/and approach and not seeing church and mission as separate is perhaps a less western and more eastern approach. Looking at churches in the UK where mission and church have become so separated, it could be said that, theologically speaking, they should not be termed 'church'. This is why terms like 'ecclesio Dei' or 'missional ecclesiology', which are inclusive of both church and mission, are more helpful ways of naming or referring to 'church.'

To help us understand better how church and mission have become so separated, we will look at the theological concepts of 'modality' and 'sodality' and the symbiotic relationship between them.

Imagine a large organisation that has a set way of doing things. It works efficiently. There is a feeling of safety and security present. However, part of the workings of this organisation involves sending teams out to engage in various 'missions'. For this they need a team of highly committed individuals who have been trained for this type of work and have been given a specific task to perform. This team takes risks, working together efficiently. This is how modal and sodal work. The organisation is the 'modal': it sustains what already is, there is stability. The crack team of highly trained individuals is the 'sodal': it is about taking risks, it has a specific task. Both modal and sodal are as important as each other, but they have different roles to fulfil. They have a mutually beneficial relationship, they are equally important and one cannot exist without the other.

So it is with church and mission, church being modal and mission sodal. Over time, the two have become separate entities and yet they shouldn't be. God uses both modal and sodal models and we need to find ways in which the two are able to work together. Of course there will be challenges and we need to hold the tension between the two dynamics.

It would be easy to see Symbiotic Youth Work as the 'going out' sodal approach where we are the ones going to the 'edges of the earth', but symbiosis moves us beyond that distinction. Church Army researcher, George Lings says, "Those liberated into sodal contexts are free to re-imagine what is needed, glad to be accountable but not controlled, and able to start what is easier to sustain".[19] It is our hope that the church, rather than viewing what we do with suspicion, sees Symbiotic Youth Work/mission as the pathfinder dissenter that stays connected relationally to the modal. However, it is of itself neither modal nor sodal. Rather it is beyond these thought types and a church/community feeling its way into a new way of being and doing. As we have discussed, as soon as you begin to define, to try and shape what it is we are doing, it loses its potency. To define youth work and mission as sodal is problematic as it immediately insinuates a separation with the modal idea of church. What we are doing takes on the very qualities of the landscape it inhabits and is, therefore, unclear, unknown and indefinable.

To help us envision this further, let's draw on an analogy rooted in nature (as symbiosis is). There is a plant in the Sahara desert called the 'resurrection plant'. Rather than being fixed in place, it blows about the sand looking for what scant water it can find, waiting for the rain which then 'resurrects' it. It then drops its seeds and new plants grow. These plants in turn dry out and are blown by the wind again to search out water. Where it grows is not set, fixed, planned or bounded.

We are more used to a more modal type of garden landscape where plants are cultivated and nurtured into a particular design that grows and becomes a fixed beautiful garden. Any 'wrong' plants are weeded out. Something like a wild meadow might be seen as more of a sodal garden concept. Whilst the meadow has been allowed to develop naturally, it is bounded by barriers to stop it spreading where it is not wanted.

In contrast to our designed garden and our meadow, the resurrection plant journeys to seek out new places in the landscape. It is not tethered and goes where the wind blows. It is very different. It is neither modal nor sodal. None of these plants or environments

1

is better than the others, they are just different, adapting to differing landscapes and perhaps, in the case of the resurrection plant, doing unexpected things that (modal/sodal) plants don't usually do.

As we begin our symbiotic journey, we do so with our newly packed kit bag but also we walk within a framework of 'being', a mind-set, a 'theological hoodie' if you will. We encapsulate this mind-set from the very beginnings of our journey. The key ideology of this is that of 'habitus' – a notion which we have been exploring in StreetSpace since 2008. It is not a new concept, but one discussed here to further aid our understanding.

Why we act like we do

Bourdieu, a French sociologist and philosopher, helped develop the concept of habitus.[i] Habitus refers to how the dispositions of, for example, home life, social standing, historical imperatives, class and ethnicity come together to form the context and the environment we grow up in. These dispositions influence how we think, behave and determine the choices we make. They have grown out of the conscious and unconscious actions of both our childhood influences of family and the environment we have grown up in (nurture versus nature). However, what makes habitus distinctive as a concept is that these dispositions change and adapt as we mature. Therefore, our habitus both exists (in its primary form as developed in childhood) and is evolving (as we grow and encounter new situations). It is neither free will, nor about determined absolutes but is a combination of the two. Habitus recognises that our cultural context is a two-way street: we both exist within a social framework influenced by social and familial structures, but are also able to influence these ourselves, creating our own habitus.

To help us understand what this looks like (the existing and evolving element of habitus) Bourdieu uses the analogies of sport and jazz to further define it. In jazz, the player needs to be familiar with their instrument in order to experiment (or jam) with other musicians. To play a game of sport, you have to know the rules but also have a 'feel' for the game, an instinctive response. So here we see how the primary habitus (that learnt in childhood) gives us the foundation in which to experiment in the development of our own habitus.

Bourdieu suggests that habitus is more than just our participation within the structures of society. He believes our interactions with society contribute towards the unfolding 'habitus': that it is a two-

---

[i] See Bourdieu (1984).

way concept of both existing and evolving; a two-way dialogue or interactive process. It is not about standing at a distance and observing, but rather an immersion. This is the habitus we are trying to create with Symbiotic Youth Work.

However, powerful institutional forces can restrict the extent to which our engagement with them is interactive. In turn, this impinges upon any two-way development. Due to the power of the established view of church – even in the light of the unfolding experiences of practitioners – little has changed in the dominance of institutional 'church'. Even though much has been said about the need for church and mission to be more closely linked, the language and practices of the mainstream (dominant structural habitus) continue to enforce the divide. What we have managed to do, by both challenging the established view of what church is and by engaging in its own unfolding story (a symbiotic approach), has been to create a space for a participative habitus which is more reflective of the existing and evolving concepts proposed by Bourdieu.

Graham, Walton and Ward[20] argue that, in order to rebuild a Christian theology that is more in line with the spirit of the Gospel, we must first identify where the Christian tradition has drifted away from the Gospel and redevelop a more liberating theology. It is equally important that this is accompanied by a liberating story that enables people to imagine and cultivate a new approach to church. The symbiotic missional approach of StreetSpace is one such story.

So how do you co-produce new forms of Christian community symbiotically with young people in contemporary culture? Alan Richardson suggests, "All Christian doctrine arises from Christian experience".[21] Our experience also gives a context for developing a doctrine and possible theology. While I am not suggesting that symbiosis is new doctrine, it is an approach that is rooted in experience. As people follow the missio Dei today, they find their mind-set and theological positioning are challenged. As people become more and more involved in this post-modern, post-Christendom context, they recognise that fresh approaches are needed. Often, however, they lack the theological underpinning in which to frame their desire to see new things happen. When we are given alternative frameworks that have strong theological roots and that are practice (story) driven, it allows us to follow new paths alongside these evolving experiences as they happen. Symbiotic Youth Work is one such framework that has developed through our work with StreetSpace. Our theological reflection on this work – the notion of seeing church as both being and doing – recognises that

1

church and mission are synonymous; that as you engage in mission you are being church with the people around you (whether they choose to believe or not).

Emerging church practitioners rarely have difficulties in relating to people, but the overarching structures and church beliefs remain problematic. They are imbued with notions of power which are a barrier to some people outside of church and a dynamic the church will struggle to liberate itself from if left to its own devices. However, when we reject the notion of mission as a bridge into church and instead grasp the idea of being and growing church, we approach church from the powerless position revealed to us through the example of Jesus: a place where all belong and have direct access to G-d, because when Jesus breathed his last the curtain was torn and we are allowed into the holy place (Mark 15: 37-38). Only in that place can something genuinely new begin to emerge. As this missionary approach unfolds and is shaped by all who are present and participating, something is co-produced to which all can belong, held not by false boundaries but instead by relationship and values.

A shared journey

As mentioned previously, there is a philosophical term, that might be helpful in enabling us to grasp what this shared mutual journey of discovery might look like. It was given spiritual resonance by 20th century Russian thinkers. That term is 'sobornost'.

Sobornost refers to unity, co-operation, freedom and community between individuals as they develop a spiritual relationship in which they act as one unit of fellowship without sacrificing their individuality. This is like a perfect loving family, where everybody is an individual but each exists, sacrifices and works together for a unified aspiration and mutual benefit. Rowan Williams discusses the term a number of times in his study of Eastern Orthodox theologians.[22] In relation to the emerging church, the notion of 'sobornost' offers a third way and a helpful theological backdrop, which is rooted in the Christian tradition, to the symbiotic unfolding/evolving habitus: a co-producing approach to ecclesiology and community.

A central idea behind the emerging church initiative is that we follow the missio Dei and journey with those who are not Christians. We share with them our beliefs and thesis, but their opposing ideas or antithesis, voice, culture and context help us to liberate the church from what it has become. Out of this, a new way of being emerges as we journey together towards a life in all its fullness, something sobornost affirms. Whilst many will grapple or be challenged by the concept of unbelievers influencing what church is and becomes, sobornost hints at a Christian tradition where genuinely inclusive and reciprocal mission is located and liberation can begin.

This sobornostic approach was behind what was termed 'Curry Church'. This was portrayed in the BBC documentary *Does Christianity have a future?* which was aired in April 2011 and featured StreetSpace Chard. Over a curry with young people we explored, through the use of the FaSt game,[i] the story of the prodigal surfer (based on Luke 15:11-32). The documentary showed a few key moments of young people breaking bread, engaging in story and experiencing fellowship. At one point the joker of group, reflecting on the story, walked the length of the table to apologise to another young person he had pushed too far earlier in the week and sought his forgiveness.

In this type of Symbiotic Youth Work, contextualised stories have become a key tool for the reimagining of church. In StreetSpace we try to re-imagine Biblical stories with the help of our *Bible, Culture* and *Tradition* compass in ways that help young people share the journey. This story illustrates this approach:

> *Charlie was a BMXer who loved riding and loved the adventure of riding close to the edge and pushing new tricks. She was quickly developing a reputation as an excellent rider, so in order to make the most of her growing profile, she decided to set up a shop locally and online and develop a brand of clothes and equipment. Her technical skills grew and meant she could design new pedals and peripheral equipment that really enhanced riding and made the whole experience more enjoyable. She even invested in new technology, such as new alloys that could be used in frames, and was soon making frames that were lighter and stronger than anything else on the market. She made sure that everyone working for her got a fair wage and used ethical suppliers where possible. Charlie was quickly raking it in, but she remained the same person as always as the money didn't corrupt her. She gave a portion away to those who needed it and always tried her best to be honest in business.*
>
> *The thing she loved about having money was still rooted in*

---

[i] The FaSt game was originally developed as a discipleship tool. It is not a competitive game but encourages people to tell their stories, to listen to and draw from other people's experience of life and in a way that impacts the world around them. For more information undertake an internet search for 'FaSt Game Richard Passmore'.

adventure; only now she could travel to loads of places around the country and abroad. She flew around the world and rode in well know places that were but distant dreams to many. On returning from her travels, she paid attention to business and things continued to grow, but she was never quite satisfied and always longed for something else.

At about the same time a man was travelling around the area; he also had a growing reputation. People weren't quite sure what to call him; he wasn't a skater or biker. Some people called him the 'Well-digger', as he once helped people find some water and dig a well. Some people called him the 'Builder' for similar reasons. Others called him 'Sufi' – someone who was spiritually enlightened and at peace with themselves. To others he was the 'Storyteller'. The problem was he never fitted into any one box. People who had heard his stories or spent time with him could never sum him up in one word, or label him 'this' or 'that'. They said that he had healed the sick and helped the poor, built houses, that you never knew what was going to happen next with him, and that although he too was poor, he was rich in a different way. The group that travelled around with him were known as 'the adventurers', because he set them challenges and always asked questions that made them think or act in a different way. As a group they never knew where they were going next or what they were going to have to eat the next day, but something always turned up – and anyway, what better way to keep the adventure real?

Even though Charlie had been on many adventures and always pushed her riding to the next level, she always felt something was missing. Something needed to change, she told herself, and so she went to find this man that couldn't be put in a box. Finding him, and not being the shy and retiring type, she explained how she loved the adventure and how she had tried to live an ethical life and asked, "What must I do to join the adventurers and journey with you?"

The man replied, "Go and sell all your possessions, your business, your bikes and inventions and give the money to the poor. Then come and join us." Charlie went away disappointed.

Here is one example of a re-contextualised story. You may recognise it as the story of the rich young ruler (Mark 10:17-22) discussed earlier, contextualised for the young people to engage with. We left this story on the tables at the restaurant where we meet with young people once a month at M&Ms (meals and meetings). Some young people picked up the story and read it whilst others asked us to tell them the story. Some engaged with the process, whilst others did not. We did not explain the story but entered into discussion with them, allowing the story to speak to the young people and us. This approach does not rely on a pre-determined understanding of the story or formulaic approach to what is meant by it.

An ever-present God

All too often we can reduce our understanding and theology to a formula. We might see God as 'transcendent', above and beyond all. Alternatively we might see God as 'imminent' and close at hand. As we attempt to get our heads around God, it can be tempting to see things in some sort of formulaic way where God is either out there and beyond or close by and intimate. However, G-d is both – and also beyond all of these considerations. Another example of applying some sort of formula to G-d is the use of popular phrase 'What Would Jesus Do (WWJD)'? We have somehow come to reduce the greatest ethical teacher to four words on a wristband and we think that, because of this, we understand and would know what Jesus would do. Likewise, we can approach the Bible in a similar formulaic way where we tell and teach whilst others listen, seemingly unable to unfold the stories mutually with young people. However, when we do, when we see something new emerge – as we described earlier with the illustration of the wedding banquet in the previous chapter – it can be an enlightening sobornostic experience.

Pete Rollins,[23] suggests the mystic tradition teaches that God is imminent: so close that we cannot see Him, so close that you lose focus. There are times when God is imminent and times when He is transcendent – God becomes hyper-real in this process. Desire is not born in the absence of God, but in the presence of God and this is something we have to discover for ourselves. It is learning to hold the tension of the imminent and transcendent that enables you to move freely as you journey into the Land of Dragons. It is too easy to become locked into the particular 'special moment' that happens and see this as the only way. For example, it was the transcendent nature of G-d that helped us recognise the imminence of Flow and enabled us to move on with G-d beyond Flow once that group had matured. Rollins likens transcendence to being in a coffee shop waiting for your partner: you are sitting and there is an empty space next to you; you are expecting your partner. They are no less real because they are not there. Symbiotic mission recognises this in the

1

journey with young people. God is no less real in the transcendence than He is in the imminence. If you focus just on the transcendence you lose some of the imminence and vice versa.

Kester Brewin[24] challenges us to embrace the 'other'. He argues that church should be a "third place", not necessarily a comfortable or familiar place, but a space where we can meet the 'other' and be prepared to face ourselves, as well as our known and yet-unknown God:

> "Christianity then is not a religion of exclusivity, of a predestined group who are chosen for salvation. Instead it is the set of those who know/embrace this paradox of being strangers. We are the boundary, not the centre, we are the other, not the included, and it is out of this realisation that our empathy for the oppressed and marginalised springs."[25]

In engaging with Symbiotic Youth Work, we encounter the 'other' in young people. In doing so, we continue to journey towards the divine. It could be argued that our work with young people, with its unfolding, fluid, evolving nature, will always embrace the 'other' within the church, society, the young people and ourselves –this creates a symbiotic context.

So, symbiotic mission becomes the response to the God-event: our response to being embraced by the Father, encountering his Son and being engaged by the Spirit in the on-going dance with the community we are part of. Too often it is people's experience and view of church that shapes mission rather than how they see Jesus in the light of this.

We can thus see Symbiotic Youth Work in action through the developments discussed so far with Flow, leading to church of Flow, and onto Curry Church. As we engaged young people with Flow, we created a symbiotic community that has been changed and shaped as we journeyed with young people. Developing community in this symbiotic way is not necessarily about a geographical sense of place, but about how to unfold a new way of being community and Kingdom. Presently, the temporariness of Curry Church has finished; something new is now emerging, like a piece of paper unfolding, which is replacing Curry Church. We don't know what is going to happen in the future, but it is the unfolding process that is important, the emergence. The young people have a heart for their community and therefore a sense of openness and awareness to see what comes next.

Changing the pace

One of the ways we are engaging in Symbiotic Youth Work practice is by drawing on skills of 'pacing'. Although similar to the idea of animation in youth work (as discussed earlier), 'pacing' is derived from the reading of body language as a tool for working with young people displaying aggressive behaviour. This involves using your own body language to change the 'pace' of an encounter with a group of young people. For example, in a street context with young people who are standing around being aggressive, the worker can change the pace of the encounter by sitting on the pavement curb. This change of body language and position shifts the dynamic and, in particular, changes the power relationship being experienced. In some ways it puts the worker in a more vulnerable position, but in reality it alters the dynamic to such an extent that space is created for something different to happen.

We also developed Symbiotic Youth Work through the use of pacing language and creative methods to create new spaces. This changes the horizon with the young people and this notion of pacing is another useful tool for your kit bag. For example, in our work we will often use the word 'church' to pace a space and connect to the missio Dei. In practice, youth workers often find themselves engaging young people in spaces that are unique, holy or accepting. Most youth workers can think of a time, either on a residential or during some encounter with young people, where a significant moment has happened (the Celts used to call this a 'thin place' where heaven and earth seem closer together). These momentary glimpses can be opened up through the use of language to pace that space. Whether in those thin moments or in the context of an established relationship, good use of questions and conversation can create a dialogue around what is happening at that moment, which sets the historical context of what has been achieved into a symbiotic paradigm. Asking a group of young people, when you feel you are in a thin place, "Is this spiritual? Does this feel like church? Could this be church?" and questions of a similar nature can aid reflection and the co-creation of community together. (Obviously it would be possible to use such questions in a purposed dominant way to achieve the workers' particular agenda. However, this is counter to the values we discuss and unpack further in the next section of the book).

It is important to recognise the role power plays in pacing, the unfolding mission and how we seek (in Symbiotic Youth Work) to dissipate this power as much as possible. Inevitably in the early

1

stages of any youth work, the power is more vertically orientated and often rests with the worker. However, as the relationship grows it can be moved towards a more equal power relationship. Essentially you are flattening out the power relationship and risking the relationships that have been built so far as you pace and change the relationship over time.[i]

Pacing does not happen within a vacuum, but is drawn from the culture of the young people with whom you are engaging. Your skills as a youth worker, your resources as a human and your own cultural upbringing can help move this to a more symbiotic relationship. We need to recognise the power and context that we come from and try to work within a more balanced framework.

Symbiotic Youth Work allows us to re-imagine and co-create church within this space, drawing from all the points of the compass (*Bible*, *Culture*, *Tradition*), and enabling young people to be fully active and co-operative in that process. This is easier said than done. Often workers find themselves within Christian traditions and structures that bring a more pre-determined purpose and dominance into the context. For example, there may be the pressure to get young people into the church, and this in turn has a gravitational pull away from the *culture* of young people towards a Christian *tradition* or a particular interpretation of the *Bible*.

For those of you who are beginning to wonder if embracing Symbiotic Youth Work might be heretical, we would simply say that, even if it is, the heretical imperative has a place within the Christian tradition! For example, during the reformation Martin Luther was widely regarded as a heretic as he sought to re-imagine what the Bible might be saying: his teaching is now seen as an orthodox traditional Christian approach. Yesterday's heresy is often today's orthodoxy and such matters need to be carefully considered.

Symbiosis in Practice

Throughout this section we have identified a number of conditions that can act as a resource to promote symbiotic practice. These include ideas that:

- **'Truth' is a moveable feast**. Here we reinforce the need for missional humility, countering Christendom arrogance – the idea that we somehow know it all. Mission

---

[i] This is demonstrated in Section Three where we explore the Nine Stages and facilitate a move from 'basic small group work' to 'risky small group work'.

1

is about following the missio Dei, the magnetic force of our compass, which is a dynamic and enlightening process. Christianity is a faith that questions our answers to enable us to journey together. Rather we see through the glass 'dimly', that we may find our liberation. If we listen to other people's truth, they will listen to our story. The young people we walk alongside can be our guides in this new land. As familiar inhabitants they can offer us a unique insight into the lay of the land, the stories, the language, the taboos, the traditions and customs. The young people can assist you on your travels and, as your relationships develop, eventually become companions on your journey.

- **Mission is worship**. Like the bridge between church and mission has been collapsed as we examine the Bible and delve into the Christian conditions, we see mission and prayer as a way of life rather than something we do at a particular time in a particular place. Like a torch that illuminates our path, this fuels our faith and allows us to engage with the people.

- **The challenge of power**. The new unfolding mission/church as a process itself might challenge the powerful position of the institutional church. The reciprocal nature of our approach balances out any bias towards the powerful. We lay aside our power and we walk into the new land, not with implements to bludgeon those we encounter, but with instruments to navigate with.

- **It is all relative**. The relativity of post-modern culture opens up dialogue and listening to others that in turn offers and reinforces the desire for relationships – a good place to start a journey of discovery! Like all good explorers, we go in with our eyes and ears open.

- **Hyper-criticism is important**. Post-modernity has deconstructed a lot of what has gone before. However, if seekers seek, they will find. Therefore, we need to strap on some all-terrain footwear that allows us to step outside of our conditioning to liberate the church and ourselves – to encourage questions rather than simply giving answers.

At Greenbelt, youth workers were recently asked what the three

1

most important words in missional youth work were. The reply was simple: 'courage, courage, courage'. We must have the courage to value the *culture*, to value the *tradition* and to value the *Bible*, and the courage to re-imagine community that is symbiotically developed with the young people we serve.

Section 2:
Resources for the Road

2

Chapter 5 – Don't be Scared of Dragons

In this section, we unpack what the Land of Dragons is and consider how we can best prepare ourselves for what lies ahead on our journey. This includes exploring the values and principles of good youth work and why these are important for the work we are participating in. We are going to find ourselves in situations where we feel uncomfortable or out of our depth, but if we are willing to take the risk the effect can be far reaching.

> *If you have ever watched Father Ted, you will remember that Mrs Doyle often asks, "Will you have a cup of tea?" Well, that is what happened to me when the dad of one of the young people we knew well had invited us in for tea several times. Being quite new to youth work at the time and not sure of the protocols, it seemed difficult to refuse the repeated invitations. We were nervous about going in knowing he was bringing up three children by himself; two of whom were young lads we regularly encountered on the street often slightly the worse for wear! It would have been easy to make an excuse because we weren't sure what lay on the other side of the door, but sitting down for a cuppa cemented a relationship with a family that has lasted for decades and seen colleagues continue to work with the family and go into the house for that elusive cup of tea.*
> **Richard Passmore**

Standing in the gap

Figure 2 is a representation of the Christian faith journey and is based upon Jonny Baker's reflection[i] on the work of Catholic theologian, Gerald Arbuckle (whose thinking about 'dissent' we have already discussed). It illustrates a process in which we become caught up in the *Founding Story* (1) of Christianity/faith, perhaps indicative of first becoming a Christian, when you are fired-up and full of the possibilities. We then come to *Reality* (2) as we seek to put into practice the story with others and discover that perhaps not all is what we were expecting. We are so embraced by the *Founding Story* that this creates an *Energy (and desire) for Change* (3). However, as we start that process, challenges come our way and we end up being led through our own *Personal Gethsemane* (4), where we re-evaluate a lot of what is happening around us and grasp a *Growing New Reality* (5) of the story, until eventually we begin to enter into a *New (understood) Reality* (6). We can probably all pinpoint where we currently are on this journey. Grappling with change and trying to work out for ourselves what this *New Reality*

---

[i] Presented at a Church Mission Society training session in 2013.

will look like generates fuel for the journey and creates a climate of openness to others, thus developing the right conditions to foster Symbiotic Youth Work.

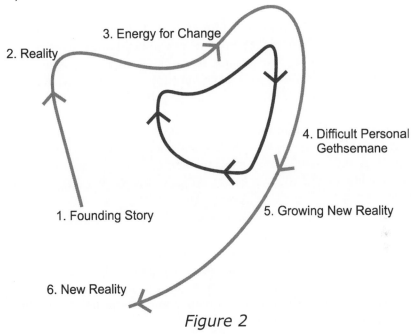

Figure 2

What this essentially illustrates is that pioneering youth workers, ministers, or change-makers of any kind find themselves in a gap between the *Founding Story* and the present *Reality* of the work. This is even more prevalent for youth workers in the changing society and culture we have around us.

When we discussed this process at a recent StreetSpace Gathering, it was clear that many of us are faced with a *Reality* that makes us question our beliefs. The gap between the *Reality* we encountered and what we had initially believed forced us to return to the Gospel stories. What was also clear is that this type of process is not a 'one time' process but a continual cycle (shown in the looping inner circle). As we move through it, there are highs and lows: firstly catching glimpses of the *New Reality*; next identifying connections between this and the *Founding Story*; then re-evaluating the *Founding Story* in the light of this *New Reality* as you journey with young people. Having journeyed through this personally, and been around many other fellow travellers, we recognise that it can be frightening and lonely, often compounded by the uncertainty of not yet knowing the *New Reality*.

The prospect of this *New Reality* being located in a Land of Dragons is scary. We are entering a place we have never been before. We could adapt a well-known quotation you may recognise and say: "The Land of Dragons, the final frontier. These are the voyages of (insert your project name)! It's continuing mission: to explore strange, new worlds...to boldly go where no man has gone before".

As we explained earlier, the analogy of the Land of Dragons is that the dragons are not 'literal', but represent a place of mystery, the unknown. The only way we can find out for ourselves what this new landscape is like is to 'boldly go'. As we journey we find that perhaps this place of 'dragons' isn't really that scary after all. The encouragement is that the process illustrated above acts a bit like an ever-decreasing circle, with the gap between the *Founding Story* and the present *Reality* narrowing: the more you embrace this as a spirituality of the road, the less difficult (but no less painful) the *Gethsemane*.

A good illustration of someone experiencing this process is Steve Blower (a member of the StreetSpace community based in Birmingham) through his work with the 'the Wildstyle Disciples'. The following example is from his research paper *Towards A B-boy Theology*.[26] Steve runs dance classes in b-boying, a form of street dance that has its roots in the hip hop culture. Participants are called b-boys or b-girls or breakers.

> When I began the dance classes two years ago they were followed by a Bible reading group for anyone who was interested in staying. Most of the young people did stay, and engaged to some degree. In a sense this was a very positive thing, the young people had opportunity to develop mentally, physically, emotionally and spiritually through this varied program, and yet something about the process itself seemed disjointed and contrived, inferring that there was no real connection between the activity of dancing and the Bible reading sessions.
>
> At my most critical, I saw it as a means of attracting young people to the message of the Gospel by doing something fun and culturally acceptable. In its crudest form, like giving young people a spoonful of sugar to help the Gospel medicine go down. Such an approach makes two problematic assumptions; that the Gospel is dull, and that b-boying is not concerned, or imbued, with something of God.[27]

Steve was looking for a way in which he could connect the Gospel with the culture of the young people he was working with, searching for a way of authentically integrating mission and culture in a more symbiotic relationship. The young people, or 'Wildstyle Disciples', started discussing various issues in their 'Social Ciphers', which mimicked the dance ciphers[i] the young people participated in as part of their dance class. These social ciphers ran after the dance classes Steve led. Steve goes on:

> The process undertaken raised some significant new insights with regard to my local setting, but also more widely to the practice of youth ministry. The research has affirmed the depth of b-boy culture, the value and relevance of the Gospel among young people and the congruity between the two. This indicates more broadly that Christian teachings can be understood within cultural activities.
>
> Overwhelmingly, b-boying has been identified as beneficial in developing theological ideas among young people whilst intrinsically valuing the culture itself. The broader implication here is that youth ministry need not misuse culture as a tool for evangelism but can instead openly celebrate those aspects that reflect Christ. Such an approach allows for expression of the Gospel message without manipulation or coercion.[28]

This finding is of particular importance if such work engaging marginalised young people in theological dialogue and spiritual development is to be of any lasting value. As many will not have come from any form of Christian tradition, the dialogical approach will help the young people really grapple with the story and their own spiritual development and so integrate it into their lives. It will be a radical and courageous shift for the church to embrace such a dialogical, practical and integrated approach to theology because this can challenge so much of what has gone before. However, it is also necessary, as we move to a more post-Christian, post-modern society, to ensure relevant expressions of church in the future.

Expecting the unexpected

In 2002, the former United States Secretary of Defence, Donald Rumsfeld was talking about the very serious subject of possible weapons of mass destruction in Iraq. He said, now rather infamously, that:

- There are known knowns; there are things we know that we know.

- There are known unknowns; that is to say, there are things that we now know we don't know.

- But there are also unknown unknowns – there are things we do not know we don't know.

---

[i] A cipher is when people gather in a circle with space in the centre to 'battle' or perform against one another.

On the commencement of our journey we have 'known knowns', which include knowing that we will encounter young people who inhabit a different culture to ours, who will use different language to us and who have differing views of the world. There are the 'known unknowns'; that we don't really know what to expect on our journey or where it will take us. Finally, there are the 'unknown unknowns'; those things that we will learn along the way (especially from the young people themselves) that will soon become a shared reality as we journey symbiotically together. To help us with all of these considerations and encounters, we have our kit bag that we can delve into for resources.

Trust your instincts. We all are made in the image of God. He sent his son Jesus to be amongst us, to relate to us, to be one of us. So must we go amongst the young people we work with. Relationship is the key, as we have previously discussed noting Symbiotic Youth Work as a move on from the relational and incarnational youth ministry that came to the fore in the mid-1990s. Building relationship with the young people can be hard work, but journeying with them through the good and bad is part of the redemptive process. We may not know what we will find, but perseverance and commitment to the journey are needed, no matter where the path leads us, because that's all part of the adventure!

Overlaying all of this is the pursuit of sobornost: what goes before, what is present now, and what we seek for the future. As you pursue the adventure, you are creating a new way of growing and being church with the young people you work with. You are instigating this habitus from the very beginning of your journey – that together you are creating something new and evolving. It is important to be open to this as you journey into the Land of Dragons.

Immersion in the 'now'

It has been argued that sense is made of the world by considering a thesis (i.e. a proposal, explanation or proposition about what 'might be') and an anti-thesis (an alternative view or reaction to the original thesis) in order to achieve synthesis (a way of resolving the conflict between the original thesis and the anti-thesis). In our western world, there is often the desire to perceive things through different lenses, pulling them together into a synthesis to develop understanding which, in our context, then informs our youth work. The problem is that this instantly implies a distancing between youth worker and young people, or that it is the worker as 'the expert' that draws the strands together to form the synthesis. This sits uncomfortably with the roots of Symbiotic Youth Work. The introduction of symbiosis brings us to a new place and offers us an equal and mutual approach to working with young people. Through this pursuit of relationship with 'other', we go beyond looking at things through a lens, we go beyond synthesis. This co-operation or collaboration with all (youth worker, young person, community, humanity, creation, God and G-d) allows us to see what will unfold: it is the sobornost or third way, the evolving yet existing habitus. Through symbiosis, the work we engage in becomes an immersion in the 'now' and 'not yet', not merely an observation, or something we can 'think' out.

Part of this new way of being is understanding the importance of temporary spaces: where new forms of community can be unfolded for a limited time in a particular place but will have wider repercussions and help us grow in our understanding of what community means. These make the powerful powerless, allowing us to be real, to move, flow, tack with what is happening rather than plan what is to happen. We become pilgrims.[29] This embracing of the temporary goes against the permanence of structure that we associate with church and helps us move with the imminence and transcendence of G-d. Don't be afraid of the temporary. We might feel we have to make church happen all the time and build something big and concrete. Strong and structured is beautiful, but sometimes we need to be tent-dwelling nomads, pitching our tent and then departing when the time is right. Within the work of StreetSpace we have discovered that temporary spaces are important and should be embraced, not feared.

In his essay, *T.A.Z. The Temporary Autonomous Zone, Ontological Anarchy, Poetic Terrorism*,[30] Hakim Bey discusses temporary moments akin to, say, an uprising (rather than a revolution, which is more about creating permanent change – and often does not live up to the dreams or ideals of the revolutionaries) or to moments of community that may emerge in a music festival.

There is no permanence. No matter how challenging, stimulating and energising, you wouldn't want festival conditions every day. (Endless mud and wet wipes? No thank you!) Even so, the temporary experience can affect profound change. T.A.Z. moments can appear and disappear, like guerrilla gardeners planting the seeds that emerge later for another moment of temporary liberation.

We were preparing to take a group of young people out to Romania to rebuild a local pharmacy. The aim was to help the local community in Romania and give the young people some work experience. In order to make the trip possible we needed to raise quite a bit of money and so a meeting was called to discuss the fundraising plans. Little did we know at the time

*that the local motorcycle group had signed up to support us
so, on answering my front door on the evening of the meeting,
it was a shock to discover three tattooed grizzly bikers who
joined the meeting with a few parents and young people. The
space quickly shifted from a foreign space as we shared ideas
and hatched a plan. It was hard to work out why the space
was so special but it was certainly a T.A.Z in the making.*
Richard Passmore

A T.A.Z moment is not always planned, but can arise. A T.A.Z. is
fleeting and, before it can become a described entity, it will
disappear. With this comes great freedom to create all types of
temporary experiences without the pressure of permanence,
structure or definition. T.A.Z. spaces need not be physical, but can
also be 'virtual' through the use of social media. This is particularly
relevant to detached work and the way we engage with the young
people we work with. T.A.Z.s are a great example of Symbiotic
Youth Work and mission unfolding in action. They mirror the
journeying, incultural approach that we mentioned earlier where you
need to let go of your notions of truth and relax into a space in the
hope that something special emerges. Too often we think we are
journeying like this with young people when in fact we are more like
sixteenth century explorers, such as Cortez, holding on too tightly to
our notions of fixed truth and story. We may not be forcing people to
believe certain things or beating people into submission, but by not
genuinely being open-handed with the truth, our positional power
and dominance can pollute the space and hinder any genuine
newness emerging.

There are countless times in youth work when we know a particular
course of action would help a young person, but also know that if we
suggest that course of action they will reject it. Instead we need to
help them arrive at the answer themselves. It is the same with the
unfolding spirituality.

*At the end of our skate and bike pilgrimage, we stopped off for
lunch near a church with a Celtic cross. It had ornate carvings
of Celtic knots that, to me, obviously spoke of Flow being
weaved in and out of life. The temptation to explicitly point this
out to the young people and make all the connections for them
was hard to resist. However, the value of them recognising
how Flow connected to the Christian tradition for themselves
as they traced the knots with their fingers was immeasurable.*
Richard Passmore

Equally, Steve (with the b-boy/girl dancers) illustrates that by being open-handed, immersed in the context, and developing an understanding of it, something new can emerge. Youth culture is fluid, ever-changing and the young people are transient. The groups of young people you engage with will change over time as they get older, move away or change interests. In Section 3 we discuss how groups play a really important role. It would be easy to individualise youth work and only measure the growth of individuals, but in doing so we could lose the possibility of T.A.Z's emerging and the importance of community unfolding.

T.A.Z's will pop up from time to time and our best hope is to create the conditions where T.A.Z's can emerge. Therefore, we need to be continually evaluating and observing the groups we are part of. Like a surfer waiting for a wave, see the change coming and prepare. We would advocate that work which may have been very successful and reaped a lot of rewards for you and the young people may need to be closed down, in mutual agreement with them, if it has run its course. Like a river, we go with the flow of the water. When we need to rest, we do so in a still spot at the side on the riverbank or in a shallow pool. We know, however, that this is not the end of our journey and at some point we will once again enter the flow of the river. While we rest, we watch for the signs that will show us when the right time to re-enter is.

God is already there

Symbiotic Youth Work is itself informed by the term 'missional community', which is gathering more use in emerging church circles. It describes a way of emulating Christ, who focussed on openness and approachability, not only to those on the margins of society, but also those at the centre. The word 'missional' is used rather than mission to reflect the missio Dei, and to set it apart from traditional approaches to mission that are often an aspect of institutional church life, or an action of church, rather than 'being' church. In the past, we have used the term 'missional ecclesiology' to try and give a sense of the emerging community of church. This description is about a group of people journeying together: journeying with Christ and with each other; those who are believers and those who are not; those at the core and those at the edge or on the margins.

Symbiotic mission recognises that God is already here and there: God is already hanging out with the young people, and asking, "Where were you?" What we need to do is get in on God's act, rather than try and direct or forge our own path. Just as Jesus only did what he saw his Father in heaven doing, so must we seek out what God is already doing amongst the young people we work with.

Chapter 6 – Values-Led Practice

Broken relationships

This notion of symbiosis encourages a values-led practice, exploring further our own issues, processes, relationships, attitudes and priorities. Ultimately the Gospel is a story and the Bible is a narrative about the relationship between God, humanity and creation; the damage to that relationship and the attempts at restoring it. What we see in the Bible story is a breakdown of relationship at four different, but connected, levels. The one most people are familiar with, particularly those from an evangelical Christian background, is the break in relationship between God and humanity. We know the story of Jesus being about the salvation of individuals and the restoration of the personal relationship. There are old Christian tracts that focus on this, for example, using an analogy of throwing rubbish into a tunnel and causing a blockage, or of the cross spanning the gap between man and God.

However, the breakdown is much broader than this. We also see the relationship broken between humanity and creation as humanity was expelled from the Garden of Eden. Still the whole of creation yearns for redemption.

> *I consider that our present sufferings are not worth comparing with the glory that will be revealed in us. For the creation waits in eager expectation for the children of God to be revealed. For the creation was subjected to frustration, not by its own choice, but by the will of the one who subjected it, in hope that the creation itself will be liberated from its bondage to decay and brought into the freedom and glory of the children of God.* **Romans 8:18-21.**

Thirdly, there is the break in relationship within humanity itself: the way in which we relate to others and our sense of community and togetherness – or lack thereof. If shalom (as is mentioned earlier) is to happen, it can only happen within a framework of restored relationships across the whole of humanity. The recent *IF* campaign[i] highlights this well: there can be no shalom for me until there is shalom for all.

Lastly, there is the breakdown of relationship within ourselves: how we relate to ourselves and to our own humanity. In order to become fully human, in addition to being at peace with others, the world and God, we also need to be at peace with ourselves. Working towards this peace means different things to different people. Our up-bringing, background and conditioning shape our personal

---

[i] enoughfoodif.org

behaviour, some of which might need to be adjusted.

> We had noticed a group of young people aged around nine or ten who we would say "hi" to but who were not in the targeted age range of the project. However, four years later this group had become a core part of our engagement. Working with them on a regular basis, we quickly realised the high level of complex need several of these young people had. This led us to start some one-to-one work, as it was difficult to know what to say to a young person when their grandparents were the local drug dealers! We simply knew we had to get alongside these young people individually to get to the heart of the issues they were facing. The challenge of meeting the different levels of breakdown they were facing could not be under estimated. After helping them reconnect with themselves, the next step was to develop them again as a group and help them reconnect with one another.

Richard Passmore

The complexity and interconnectedness of the breakdown in these relationships should not be underestimated. It is at the root of who we are as humans and what we are trying to achieve with the young people we work with. We often talk about holistic youth work, resisting a distinction between social action and personal evangelism, but the issue is more than this and all four breakdown areas are mutually connected and interrelated. As we seek to understand values-led practice, we need to recognise that restoring these relationships is at the heart of all that we do.

Relational youth work was, and still is, often misunderstood and relationships are seen as just another tool to be used to engage with young people. When reduced to this one element, relational ministry becomes corrupted and disconnected from the heart of God that yearns for wholeness and healing at all levels. When we connect relational youth ministry to this broader restoration context and to its symbiotic distinctiveness, we begin to see a whole new way of being and existing in the Land of Dragons. We recognise that our salvation, our reconciliation to ourselves and our reconciliation to creation are bound up together as we seek to be reconciled with others. This is at the core of Symbiotic Youth Work and a core value that should underpin all that we do. From this foundation we begin to recognise that we can respond to young people and their myriad of presenting issues by drawing on wider Christian values, such as love, humility and powerlessness, that become synonymous with the core principles of youth work and actually collapse false division between youth work and youth ministry.

When our humanity is symbiotically bound up in the process of reconciliation, our work becomes a way of life, perhaps more in line with a monastic tradition or rule rather than a task to be achieved. Here again we begin to see the relationships of relational youth work as part of following the character of God and the missio Dei, rather than as a means to an end: a move beyond synthesis. This is both a joy and a problem. As youth work has moved towards outcome-driven criteria and practice, be they outcomes from local authorities, funders, government, churches or Christian organisations, it is easy to lose sight of the integral role of process.

Symbiotic Youth Work: a learning process

John Ord, in his article *The Youth Work Curriculum and the 'Transforming Youth Work Agenda'*,[31] discusses the importance of process. A curriculum system for the youth service was first introduced in the early 1990s and Ord explores curriculum as process (as first discussed by Mark Smith). Curriculum as process is about working without having pre-set outcomes and instead seeing the learning that happens as the young people and the youth workers interact. Establishing relationships, trust, voluntary participation (more so perhaps on the young person's behalf) and mutuality allow for a safe space for freedom of expression and the opportunity to explore personal and social issues. This is critical if we are to develop a curriculum as process approach.

Relationship is key to the process. Process may start with some intentionality, but is without specific outcomes in mind.[i] Indeed, as youth workers, we may not even witness the outcomes for ourselves, let alone predict what they will be. By engaging in the process, you are engaging in a 'person-centred' approach to youth work: the personal and social development of the young people you are working with. That is not to say that there will not be outcomes from engaging in the process but, as Ord says, "The learning is not accidental but incidental".[32] You may see, for example, a reduction in anti-social behaviour, which could be attributed to the work you are doing. However, you might not be able to pin-point the exact piece of work that led to this; rather it has grown out of the process of engaging in meaningful and supportive relationships with the young people you are working amongst.

With this in mind, it is important that you take on your journey the values that will create a climate for this genuine, relational youth work to take place. Meeting young people on their terms has to be a starting point for this. The recognition that our redemption is bound

---

[i] Outcomes are increasingly central to policy. We have included a chapter on *Monitoring and Evaluation* in relation to Symbiotic Youth Work in Section 4.

with theirs results in the recognition that we need to approach them from a place of humility where they are held in high regard. It is not an approach that is saying, "We have the truth in this neat little box that we are bringing to you", but it is an approach that is saying, "Will you help us together to discover what 'truth' is?" It is only from this position of humility and, as much as possible, equality that we purposefully engage in a mutually beneficial symbiotic relationship with young people. It is only from this place that we can begin a real journey of discovery with them.

As we discussed earlier in 'Unfolding Symbiotic Youth Work', recognising the role that power plays in this relationship is important. We obviously have a different power context from the young people we are working with, but the ministry modelled through the incarnation is one where Jesus puts aside much of his power, choosing to become fully human and entering into relationship with humanity.

When Moses sought the liberation of the Hebrew people, God used what Moses had in his hand – his staff (Exodus: 4:1-5). It would be wrong to assume that we should not, or cannot use the tools we have in our hand, be they increased social capital, access to resources or our time for the benefit of young people. (Nor should we underestimate our role as a mediator of a part of the story, as discussed.) But we need to do so with an empowering and participatory approach rather than a spoon-feeding, disempowering one. When we fail to recognise the power that we have and fail to dissipate that power, we fail to move in line with the symbiotic approach discussed. Good youth work has an embedded missional spirituality, whether workers recognise it or not, that is emancipatory. Poor youth ministry models simply indoctrinate.

An interesting question to raise is, "What does it mean to share the Gospel in a powerless way?" When we begin to explore this notion it brings us back to the core of Symbiotic Youth Work: that our liberation is tied to others. Likewise, when we genuinely begin to ask, "What does it mean to love young people?" we recognise that putting love into practice is a process:

> Love is patient, love is kind. It does not envy, it does not boast, it is not proud. It does not dishonour others, it is not self-seeking, it is not easily angered, it keeps no record of wrongs. Love does not delight in evil but rejoices with the truth. It always protects, always trusts, always hopes, always perseveres
>
> **1 Corinthians 13:4-7**

We recognise that as we seek to practice love in this way, we begin to learn what it means to love ourselves. It is only as we allow the interconnectedness of loving others, creation and ourselves that we can begin to fully understand what the Bible means when it says 'God is love' (1 John 4:8).

In practical terms, a lot of this boils down to simply putting young people first; allowing the outcomes to be determined by and with the young people we are serving; enabling young people to negotiate their own relationship with us; not forcing relationships by offering particular incentives (carrot and stick), but serving with an open hand. Obviously this will leave us open to being manipulated, taken advantage of and exploited. We should not be naive in recognising that at times we need to say "no" or "hold on" – but actually recognise that and saying "no" or "hold on" is all part of the redemptive, symbiotic, relational process.

Acquiescing to every demand does not form real relationships: dialogue, understanding and mutuality do. By engaging with the young people in a truly symbiotic relationship – where one cannot be whole without the others contributing to the unfolding story – real authentic relationships are formed and a new kind of church/community dynamic emerges.

Developing our effectiveness

The term 'missional spirituality' is a concept that underpins this and the next chapter. It is a term that enables the different tensions that exist within the Christian historical story to coexist. To develop a fullness of relationship, we need to recognise that there is strength in both the liberal and evangelical traditions. There is value in both Protestant and Catholic perspectives. We need to balance social action with personal evangelism, to recognise that a life journey is a series of decisions, embracing both the mystical and the concrete traditions of Christianity. Missional spirituality moves us beyond competitive arguments towards a way of being that is generously orthodox; that embraces orthopraxis and a heretical imperative when needed; that recognises that church and Kingdom are inextricably linked; that realises that the process of being church is bound up in the process of becoming human, and that old notions of who is 'in' and who is 'out' are more rooted in a power dynamic than a Gospel imperative. Of ultimate concern to God is justice and love, rather than division and loyalties to a particular view of truth. So in our context, as people called to be with young people in Symbiotic Youth Work, we hold this idea of missional spirituality and the unfolding of a new habitus together as part of an overarching dynamic.

74

In 2012, John Ord wrote a further paper about process. Entitled, *Aristotle, Phronesis and Youth Work – measuring the process: a contradiction in terms*,[33] he recognised that outcomes are produced "...through a complex set of processes and particular circumstances which unfold in practice".[34] Building on his previous article, he spoke about how 'incidental' outcomes are achieved; that they 'emerge' organically and are not necessarily planned; that they grow from engagement with young people that has purpose and intent, but is not prescriptive or planned. As is often found in youth work, it is the unexpected outcomes – ones that seem to bear little or no relation to the work – that are the most surprisingly positive. He talks about the broad aims of the youth project rather than specifics, and ones that are often implemented in conjunction with the young people themselves.

The process of journeying with the young people is key to good, effective youth work. Ord argues for a different way of conceiving youth work, one that is independent of notions of causality. This could be one of the reasons why Symbiotic Youth Work has emerged as we have reflected on the StreetSpace Nine Stage process. We identified the stages through observing practice, not because of some preconceived notion of causality. To reduce Symbiotic Youth Work to a causal process would undermine its very essence.

Practical wisdom

Ord goes on to look at Aristotle's concept of 'phronesis'. There is no modern translation of this word. Sometimes it is read as wisdom, but most frequently it is translated as 'prudence' or 'practical wisdom'. Ord notes that phronesis is about action: it is when we take all that we know, our past experience and our knowledge, and draw on this at any given moment to identify the right response to give in that situation. It is also about deciphering whether a course of action is worthwhile at all. Ord believes that phronesis helps us understand the process of youth work. Applying phronesis in this way considers the young peoples' lived experiences and what it means to live a 'good life'. Ord argues that measuring success by the outcomes they produce is not the way forward. This analysis mirrors that of N. T. Wright, who discusses how rules will only take us so far as Christians: they are helpful but we need to live with the eschatological hope as our informing construct.[35] In the same way we seek, as youth workers, to live a good life and help young people to do the same. We need to be open and accepting of a level of uncertainty when engaging young people, choosing a way that is "... more likely than not to be able to meet the unfolding and emerging needs of young people".[36]

Someone suggested that we should raise the money we needed for the trip to Romania by having a sponsored bicycle ride – cycling the equivalent distance from the UK to Romania. It seemed a good idea at the time! We liaised with the local sports centre to use their static bikes and realised we needed to keep six bikes spinning for the equivalent of 1278 miles. It quickly became apparent that with only six young people going to Romania we were going to need some help.

The event was successful in terms of achieving the target we set, but much more important had been the myriad of interactions we'd had with countless young people (including many not going on the trip) as they pitched up to take a turn on the bikes. Moments of deep discussion about healthy living sparked by the bikes were just the tip of the iceberg. We explored a host of issues and built a real sense of community with young people who freely gave of their time and effort to achieve what seemed an impossible task.

Richard Passmore

What we see here is a description of an aspect of good Symbiotic Youth Work – where the work we engage in is 'emerging' and 'unfolding'. But what Ord fails to identify here, which is what we are exploring within Symbiotic Youth Work, is the mutual relationship between young person and youth worker. It is a two-way process: it is not just about the impact it has on the young people's lives, but also how it can affect those working with them and how that close interaction leads to greater effectiveness in youth work – and in life as a human becoming.

Increasingly over the years we have seen a move towards 'professionalism' in youth work. This incorporation of outcomes can be seen with the introduction of *Every Child Matters*,[37] the content of *Positive for Youth*[38] and, more recently, the seven clusters of social and emotional capabilities put forward by the Catalyst Consortium and commissioned by the current government (see Section 4). Becoming more outcomes-driven has further imposed a gap between the youth worker and the young people they are working with. This can further distance us from a Symbiotic Youth Work approach. Ian Sparks, Chair of the Board of FYT Directors, described how a similar process had happened in social work which had led to workers becoming 'safe from everybody and open to nobody'. Youth work has adopted a professionalism that has been defined by other professions, or fields. The most obvious one is teaching.

There is a distance between teacher and pupil. There is only so much teachers can do to assist those they are working with, within the parameters of their role as teacher. This type of distancing professionalism can set limits that are counter-intuitive to Symbiotic Youth Work.

Take, for instance, a youth worker who lives in a deprived area and works with the young people on the estate where he lives. As part of this work, and to further the relationships with the young people he meets, it is a natural progression of his work that he should have an open-house policy – that allows the young people he contacts through his youth work to come to his home. This might sound risky, but with the right processes and assessments put in place, it is a natural extension of the youth work he engages in and is common place within a community where people will often be found drinking tea together in one another's houses. However, when viewing this scenario 'professionally', you would never expect a teacher to open their house to their pupils. This is where the problems lie. By laying these types of professional protocols, standards and principles over those of youth work, we see that the two don't readily match up. Applying a blanket set of processes and outcomes across differing professions is problematic. Symbiotic Youth Work goes beyond a narrow definition of professionalism to go the extra mile with young people, carefully considering each situation on its merits as it arises. To truly participate with young people, you cannot then distance yourself from them. You have to journey with them. This is what is at the heart of good youth work and what is inherently Kingdom focussed.

2

Chapter 7 – The Genetics of Symbiotic Youth Work

What we have seen, as we have begun to unfold the notion of Symbiotic Youth Work, is how rooted this is in mutual, reciprocal relationships and, for those from a Christian faith tradition, a missional spirituality. Furthermore, in this section we make connections between how all good youth and community work is, in fact, rooted in a symbiotic value system: we argue such youth work is genetically compelled to be symbiotic! We unpack the core principles of youth work (education, equality, participation and empowerment) and explore how undertaking such work in a genuinely mutual and symbiotic way is both inherently spiritual, Kingdom-orientated and well-managed. This clearly means that the application of Symbiotic Youth Work can be applied beyond a detached work context and into other youth work settings.

In the foreword to Paulo Freire's book, *Pedagogy of the Oppressed*, Richard Shaull[39] writes:

> *Education either functions as an instrument which is used to facilitate integration of the younger generation into the logic of the present system and bring about conformity or it becomes the practice of freedom, the means by which men and women deal critically and creatively with reality and discover how to participate in the transformation of their world.*

When we recognise that relationship is at the heart of what we do, we begin to see that true empowerment, education, participation and equality all forge a path towards liberation. The following story aptly illustrates what can happen when such considerations symbiotically come together:

> *In 'Meet them where they're at', we wrote about a young person who never went to school and how, when planning a trip ice skating, he had to be coached in how to use the phone to find out when the rink would be open and what it would cost etc. It took a lot of coaxing and encouragement and really basic education and confidence-building to help him do this. This young person, who was a school phobic and had attended less than fifty days of secondary education, needed constant support and encouragement to recognise the pathway that could help him change his situation. Through on-going support, he eventually found a job and was able to hold this down. Fifteen years later it was a privilege to be contacted by him via social media and discover that not only was he a father who was actively encouraging his children to attend school, but he was still in the same profession.*
> **Richard Passmore**

Core principles

The 1960 *Albemarle Report, The Youth Service in England and Wales*,[40] changed the face of youth work in the UK. After this report, the youth service was seen as a means for informal education and the report led to the youth service expanding significantly and becoming more professional, with many youth centres being built and more youth workers being employed. It gave youth work a more important role in society and put it on the government agenda, defining the purpose of youth work thus:

> *To offer individual young people in their leisure time opportunities of various kinds, complementary to those of home, formal education and work, to discover and develop their personal resources of body, mind and spirit and thus better equip themselves to live the life of mature, creative and responsible members of a free society.*[41]

In the 1990s there were further ministerial conferences[42] that stated that youth work should embody the four historic principles, which are the foundation of the work we engage in: the aforementioned education, equality, participation and empowerment. There is a strong case for claiming symbiosis between these four principles and the values we discussed in the previous chapter. We will explore each in turn and you will see the connectivity between working to these recognised principles and Symbiotic Youth Work.

Core principle: education

When we consider education, we need to be clear that we are talking about emancipatory education, not notions of 'banking knowledge'. Freire talks about 'banking' – the educative process of filling someone with knowledge. It is dictated, memorised, repeated. It is a one-way process of the teacher imparting knowledge to the student, who absorbs what is being communicated. It is not transforming or liberating.

In youth work, we engage in informal education which can take place in any setting. It can be planned (for example if your project has a requirement to raise drugs awareness), or it can be 'off the cuff'. The distinctive about informal education is that we don't know where it is going to lead before it is commenced. In a detached session, informal education will often come about through conversation; it might be helping a young person make a more informed choice or challenging their behaviour. It is not just about the worker telling the young person what to do, but educating them so that they can engage with the process. The principle behind this is that found in the well-known saying, 'Give a man a fish and he

eats for a day. Teach a man to fish and you feed him for a lifetime'.
Below are two definitions of youth work as practiced in the UK.

> Youth work is there to produce opportunities for the personal,
> social and spiritual development of young people so that they
> reach their potential outside of the school system through
> activities that they join in their leisure time. [43]

> Youth work helps young people learn about themselves, others
> and society through activities that combine enjoyment,
> challenge, learning and achievement...youth work offers young
> people safe spaces to explore their identity, experience
> decision-making, increase their confidence, develop inter-
> personal skills and think through the consequences of their
> actions. This leads to better-informed choices, changes in
> activity and improved outcomes for young people....Their work
> seeks to promote young people's personal and social
> development and enable them to have a voice, influence and
> place in their communities and society as a whole. [44]

Informal education is not about indoctrination, but about dialogue
that leads to action and reflection. We value what the young people
have to say and contribute. Within Symbiotic Youth Work, we believe
it is not just about us imparting and opening up avenues for the
young people's learning and education, but equally about how they
can affect ours as youth workers. The above definitions set youth
work within a life-affirming approach. For symbiotic practice, we
recognise that youth work is not only life-affirming for the young
people, but also for the workers.

Jesus is the great informal educator. He spoke to people where they
were, valued what they had to say and the questions they asked and
responded accordingly. He told stories and spoke in terms people
could understand, engaging them from all walks of life. He was
inclusive and respectful, and there were always opportunities to
learn. Whilst Jesus prepared himself through prayer, fasting and
spending time alone, he didn't spend hours developing resources
(except those to hand), DVD clips, flipchart paper and pens, or
inspirational songs! He was just one of the people, in the mess with
them. This is what we want you to be doing symbiotically with the
young people you work alongside.

Core principle: equality

When discussing equality as a core principle of youth and community
work, we need to recognise the distinction between ensuring that all
provision is equally accessible and that all young people have equal
opportunity to engage, and the broader equality agenda. How do we

ensure equality and inclusivity to all? There are many approaches to consider. For example:

- Multiculturalism – society is of many different cultures. Interaction within this diversity should be encouraged and, if necessary, education facilitated and information provided about it. By alleviating ignorance, you bring about more tolerance.

- Anti-racism/sexism promotes equality regardless of ethnicity or gender. We cannot change our heritage and people should not be treated differently to someone because of their different background.

- Anti-discrimination is a more all-encompassing term. It looks at the rights of all to be treated equally regardless of their age, faith, gender, ethnicity, ability, sexual orientation and social standing. Implicit within being anti-discriminatory is the recognition that some people are treated unfairly and that this needs to be addressed.

- Anti-oppression is a more focussed consideration that takes into account the views of those who are oppressed. It challenges, changes and liberates the oppressed. It employs strategies that foster participation and empowerment.[45]

The Biblical narrative features many stories of those who have been oppressed and struggled against power, from the oppression of the Israelites by the Egyptians to the persecution of the new Christians. God created the world and it was perfect: in our sinful, imperfect, fallen world, we see that, where once there was equality, now there is discord. It is a place where people are oppressed, abused and mistreated. We are called to not only love the Lord our God (Deuteronomy 6:5), but also to love our neighbour (Matthew 32:29). Through the sacrificial death of Christ, we are once more reconciled, not only to God but also to one another. We are all made in the image of God and are of one 'race' – humanity. "In Christ's family there can be no division into Jew and non-Jew, slave and free, male and female. Among us you are all equal" (Galatians 3:28-29).

We see this in the example of Jesus, who spent time with the outcasts, the misfits and those shunned because of their race, sex or disability. Jesus didn't do what society expected of him. He was motivated by love and this included challenging the injustices of the day and pursuing equality for all.

Symbiotic Youth Work includes all young people (although perhaps not all at the same time – it could be chaos!), irrespective of who they are, what they look like or where they have come from. In our symbiotic work, Jesus models an approach to equality and inclusion and, as we have previously discussed, working from an equal basis of power. We can thus see how these dynamics embrace Symbiotic Youth Work in a way that is mutual, including and offers equality of opportunity.

Core principle: participation

Participation is so strongly connected with the relational symbiotic approach that it is hard not to resist stating the obvious. Participation is about the voluntary participation of both young person and youth worker. Youth work is something young people choose to engage in. We cannot force a young person to participate against their will.

God loves unconditionally and gave us free will to choose whether to follow Him or not. This is demonstrated in the Parable of the Prodigal Son. Even though the father knows the possibility that his son will suffer, he still allows him to go and make his own choices. God advocates an open love, not a love with strings attached. The same is true of participation: we offer 'open' participation, recognising that the young person has as much right to not participate as they do to participate.

The young people we engage with are not just consumers of what we have to offer, but active participants. For example when we run M&Ms, inviting young people to participate is not just about saying to them, "Why don't you come down on a Tuesday night for a curry?" They also need to know that at M&Ms we often discuss issues and we want those who come to have the opportunity to participate in this. We also need to allow space for them to ask questions in order for them to fully understand what they are participating in so that they can make an informed decision to participate or not.

A young person who is a willing participant is much more empowered in the process and is more likely to get something out of it. For example, in our local project we have been successful in fostering integration between the young people and the local community through community fun days, fundraising and positive media reports. One day at the skate park, there was a lot of broken glass on the ground. One of the older young people saw a dog-walker and they got talking about the glass. The dog-walker offered to get a dustpan and brush and together they cleaned it up. This could only happen because of the active participation of the young people in the local community. We see here the mutual investment of the young people in the project: it is as much their project as it is ours. That is so important, not only for the young people, but also for us as a team working with them. This high level of participation was critical in fostering a symbiotic approach and beginning to unfold the new community that was emerging.

Core principle: empowerment

There will always be those with power and those without. Power comes in many guises and is described in the Oxford Dictionary online as, 'the ability or capacity to do something or act in a particular way'.[46] Power bolsters those 'with' and oppresses those 'without'.

As a symbiotic community, we strive to be interdependent: a community of individuals working together for the greater good. A common mistake people make when thinking about youth work is that youth workers are encouraging young people to be independent. However the focus should be about growing towards interdependence. We recognise the individuality of young people, but this needs to be fostered within, and through, a context of community and the interconnectedness of society. In the Gospels we see Jesus has great power: he heals the sick, preaches to the masses and has a following. Yet he was born into the world, not as a great warrior king, but as the child of a young couple miles from home and in humble surroundings. He exploded mythical expectations: he was a shepherd; the people's servant; not even death had power over him – "But God set him free from death and raised him to life. Death could not hold him in its power" (Acts 2:24).

When we think about empowerment, we do not think of giving power to the young people that we work alongside, which assumes and implies that we are already in a more powerful position than they are. Rather, we need to cultivate an environment where young people can develop and grow and be empowered. This approach enables us to both support young people and create an environment where young people can succeed (or fail), where they are willing to try. Interdependence is promoted in this context as young people take the opportunities presented and recognise that the success of the endeavour is held equally between the young people and the worker.

Unfortunately, church as we know it often disempowers young people. For the church to empower young people it needs to value them and their contribution, their vision, creativity and ideas, not just include them as a tokenistic gesture, such as allowing them to do a reading or lead the prayers once in a blue moon. This valuing is important, not just to enable the young people to feel empowered and part of the community of church, but also to give longevity to church – in order to survive we need to embrace new ideas.

We (the StreetSpace Chard team) meet together with a group of people for our own interpretation of 'church' that we call *Cakeful*. As part of this, our young daughter regularly contributes ideas (she would take over the whole thing if she could!). This level of empowerment and inclusion is something we have to wrestle with, creating a place where we can not only be inclusive, but also allow space for sharing and being open with one another. This might not always be appropriate with children around. We don't have all the answers and we are feeling our way through the process to see what evolves.

Approaches to youth work will always be discussed and many things will come and go (such as *Connexions*), but these four core principles of *education*, *equality*, *participation* and *empowerment* should, in our opinion, always remain in one guise or another as important cornerstones of youth work. We also need to ensure that these four principles are equally valued and held in tension with each other rather than be considered as four separate entities. Sometimes an approach may seem empowering, such as allowing a young person to have their own opinion, but if it is at the cost of equality, (for example they make a statement that is sexist), then we need to challenge this: this is a skilled and involved process.

It is very easy for projects to slip into a false dualism between these core principles of youth work and fail to recognise their relatedness to the Christian story. (The rise of Christian faith-based courses, which see these values as authentically Christian, has been an important contribution to the field.) However, it is also evident that the gravitational pull of a false professional ideal can manifest itself in these contexts, where boundaries are put before people and the symbiotic approach is watered down as people become experts pursuing change that is rooted in a particular perspective rather than as it mutually evolves.

Supplementary principle: unfolding group work

Finally, although not identified as one of the core principles of youth work, group work has also played an important part in the genetics of youth work: much group work theory and practice is derived from youth or social work practitioners. Groups are the context for community to unfold and emerge and are obviously central if Symbiotic Youth Work is to happen. There has been a clear drive towards individualism in youth work in recent years that has come about because of the drive towards outcomes. This is perhaps because many outcomes are easiest to measure on an individual basis.

In terms of Symbiotic Youth Work, the group work process could be described as a continued state of unfolding dialogue towards the emerging habitus. It is well recognised that groups go through a 'storming' stage as people settle into the group they are part of. Indeed, it is questionable whether, without the rigour of this storming process, if all in the group are really being heard and represented.

What we recognise in the post-modern, post-Christian context is that people inhabit a range of groups and communities and that perhaps the old concept of being highly committed to a particular group with a particular set of values needs to give way to a more 'glocal'[i] understanding of groups/community/church. In such an understanding, we symbiotically hold in tension the reality of the post-modern experience and recognise that inclusivity matters, but that particularities (such as a particular world view, a stance on the Bible or ascribing to a particular denomination) are less important than relationships.

So far we have tried to hold onto the word *church* and use it in the same breath as community. This is because we recognise the mystery of the body of Christ, that is: being and doing, passive and active, hidden and sought. It would be easy to drop the *church* word, but we recognise the Biblical emphasis that church has as the bride of Christ. Therefore, we are inclined to keep using the word in the hope that it will be redeemed and that a fresh understanding of what it really means will emerge as we move forward symbiotically.

Equally we have sought not to lose the core principles of youth work but to embrace the heart of these principles and recognise the importance they play in helping us unfold a new way of being with young people. Perhaps if we keep shouting from the edge of the canyon together, a new echo will return. At a very simple level, Rowan Williams[47] stated that church starts where Jesus is with others. Perhaps Symbiotic Youth Work is church as a mission community of dispersed people and local expressions of church with the young people alongside us – a group of people shouting together, empowering one another, learning together, being open to others and feeling our path into a new way of being – relationally connected to historic expressions of church.

---

[i] Glocal – both global *and* local

Section 3:
Stepping Out

3

Chapter 8 – Introducing the Stages

We now move from outlining the landscape of the Land of Dragons to consider how Symbiotic Youth Work is rooted in the Nine-Stage Process that we originally developed from detached work and previously outlined in *Meet them where they're at*. The thinking behind this original process subsequently expanded and we explored the concept of 'tacking' in the second publication, *Off the Beaten Track*.

For those not familiar with the Nine-Stages (and to refresh memories for those who are), the stages are:

1. Observation – finding out where the young people gather and what the area you are proposing to work in is like;

2. Cold Contact: Initial Engagement – engaging the young people for the first time;

3. Cold Contact: Extended Contact – developing your initial relationships with the young people you have engaged;

4. Area-Based Work – focusing on where you will work and with which young people;

5. Peer Group Work – building relationships with specific groups of young people;

6. Basic Small Group Work – increasing the focus, regularity and intensity of your work;

7. Risky Small Group Work – beginning to challenge the young people in a manner that promotes symbiosis;

8. Exploring Spirituality – developing ways to mutually explore faith, to intentionally raise issues of spirituality if this has not been already explicitly expressed in the previous seven stages;

9. Church on the Edge and Peer education – a mutual space where, as a group, you grow together towards community and positively impact wider society and one another.

Although the concept of Symbiotic Youth Work and mission goes broader than just detached youth work, it is important for us to explore it from this approach here, as this is where we have the broadest body of practice evidence. Therefore, this section is rooted in detached practice and still mainly discusses the stages from this setting. However, in recent years we have begun to recognise that Symbiotic Youth Work can evolve in open youth work contexts. Since the publication of *Off the Beaten Track*, we have begun to experiment with Symbiotic Youth Work in open drop-in and youth club environments. Initially we developed a Five-Stage Process for this, but more recently have successfully aligned it to the Nine-Stage design. This has evolved as we have recognised a more nuanced process was needed with more clarity between the stages.

If you work in an open youth club context, you may find it helpful to read Chapter 9 (Symbiosis in Detached Work) and consider how this relates to you in the light of your own *open* practice. As we describe the first five stages, you will find a section at the end of each which adapts our thinking for open and drop-in/youth club contexts. Stages six to nine remain the same and can be equally applied to both detached and open youth work.

The stages in the process are not a development model. They cannot be described as a clear linear strategy that will develop your work with young people from A to B in a particular time-frame. They are a reflection of what Symbiotic Youth Work looks like in practice and, to reiterate what John Ord says, they are 'incidental not accidental'[48]. Therefore, whilst we have set out a description of the stages according to our understanding and experience, each context has its own nuances and the stages need to be considered with this in mind.

Any projects interested in using the stages, either in detached work or open clubs, are welcome to contact us via www.streetspace.org.uk or www.fyt.org.uk. You will see in Section Four some of the additional benefits of using the stages in association with StreetSpace when it comes to measuring outcomes and funding possibilities.

3

Chapter 9 – Symbiosis in Detached Work

I used to love hill walking in really rugged terrain. The steeper the better; even more so if you had to scramble over rocks and boulders. The part I really liked was the isolation of hill-walking – just you and a mate walking. The best walk I have ever done was Carrauntoohil in Southern Ireland. It was a hot day and we were following a ridge-type route. The views were fantastic. The best thing about that walk was it took over ten hours and we only saw two other walkers and a sheep farmer during the whole time. When I started out in detached work in Devon, I had a similar experience: I couldn't find many young people and it took me ages to develop a group. I started in the late summer when the weather was still okay and the young people were pretty mobile, often moving on from one place to another as they got bored or received 'grief' for hanging out in that part of town.

As the town was quite spread out, most of the young people under sixteen cycled. On reaching sixteen, a 50cc moped was the thing to get (the buses were few and far between), and on reaching seventeen, the first thing they did was get a car. Consequently, the young people were often driving around, from the park to the square, up to the school and across to the rec' and a few other places in between. We would arrive at the park just in time to be informed by the younger brothers playing on the swings that they had "gone up the rec". We would walk there to discover they weren't there but had gone to the off licence. Thankfully, they were not trying to avoid me; that was just their pattern of behaviour. I thought on a few occasions that it might be more profitable to stand on the main road and jump out in front of them as they drove past! I decided I needed transport and once we resorted to driving around some of the patch, things picked up. When winter set in, I met the young people at a local pub that would let them gather there and play pool, use the jukebox and play on the arcade machine.

Richard Passmore

Detached youth work history

Historically, detached work evolved out of the early Christian mission work in poor and marginalised communities, often in cities, in the Victorian era. This work was founded by people such as Ellen Ranyard (who established the *Bible and Domestic Mission*) and Thomas Guthrie (ragged schooling) which built on the early Sunday school movement and moved on to outreach approaches, such as support work like that undertaken by the *YMCA* and *Barnardo's*. These projects developed out of a compulsion to respond to a challenging social context. From the early 1940s, contact work was developed in America and in London amongst street gangs in response to a growing moral panic. In 1960, the Albemarle report highlighted the value of detached work stating that there was:

> ... a need to experiment with peripatetic youth workers, not attached directly to any organisation or premises, who would work with existing groups or gangs of young people. [49]

In 1967, Goestchius and Tash provided further impetus for detached work in their seminal paper, *Working with Unattached Youth: Problem, approach, method*. [50]

Along with the rest of the Youth Service, detached work continued to grow in size and increase its knowledge and skills base until the 1980s when so much of the welfare system was dismantled under the Conservative Government led by Margaret Thatcher. In the early 1990s detached work increased again, although by 2004 Crimmens et al noted: "There has been a significant shift away from longer-term, area-based, projects towards short-term work with particular high-risk groups or on particular issues"[51]. Once again, it could be suggested that the increase in detached work in the 1990s was a response to a rising moral panic about young people. Negatively labelled in the 1960s as 'unattached', they had now become labelled as 'NEETs' (not in employment, education or training) in a way that necessitated fresh policy interventions. Since the millennium there has been a growing body of work around detached youth work as a distinctive approach, including publications by the National Youth Agency, the establishment of The Federation of Detached Youth Workers, and a key publication in 2008, *The International guide on the methodology of street work throughout the world*. [52]

Detached work has become a versatile, non-threatening (at least it should be!), young person-centred approach to youth work. It can be highly effective in urban and rural settings and is an important tool for working with young people who traditional youth work services would not normally come into contact with. Detached work is a style of work in which the worker goes onto the young person's 'turf': pubs, street corners, arcades or cemeteries, for example. It is based purely on relationships (as the worker is not responsible for a venue) so there is a shift in the power dynamic that allows the worker to be more flexible and responsive to the young person. This power issue is one of the reasons why Symbiotic Youth Work has primarily evolved from detached youth work. In *Can you hear the heartbeat?* Dave Andrews states:

> *Jesus advocated a radical alternative – taking control of our lives by taking control of ourselves. This alternative emphasises bringing about change by conversion – a conversion that changes us individually and collectively. It breaks the control others have over us and it rids us of the desire to control others.* [53]

Releasing control is central to Symbiotic Youth Work. This is extremely difficult to do in most 'non-detached' youth work settings, as you usually have responsibility for the venue or building.

There are two other types of youth work carried out on the streets that should not be confused with detached work. The first is 'outreach work' (not to be confused with 'evangelistic outreach'), where a worker often operates from a youth centre or club and aims to bring young people back to the base to continue working with them. They are essentially centres working in an extended way to contact young people and encourage them to attend sessions in the club. Often young people will end up becoming members and will attend regular sessions.

Work out of mobile venues, buses and caravans is also readily confused with detached work because these vehicles tend to go where the young people are. Once parked up, the workers will wait for the young people to come to them or go and invite them to use the facilities on the bus or caravan. Often the workers here will seem to be doing detached work and it is sometimes difficult to distinguish between this approach and the type of detached work we are talking about. Generally, the difference is determined by the responsibility and power dynamic of the workers. If you have young people come to any sort of venue then, as a worker, you have to be responsible for that venue, whether it is a mobile project or a purpose built centre. At some point a power and authority issue comes into play, regardless of how laid back you are about material things. If a young person decides to let off the fire extinguisher or write on the wall in the bus, you have to intervene in one way or another. You may warn them not to do it again or threaten them with a ban or other consequence for their actions. In a detached setting, a worker cannot ban a young person from, for example, the park. This is not to say a detached worker doesn't challenge certain behaviours, but this is done in the context of an equal and mutual relationship rather than out of an authority and responsibility dynamic.

In Section 4, Base Camp, we discuss the process of developing overall aims and mission statements for your work. However, as a distinct discipline within youth work, detached youth work is widely recognised to have its own aims. The original aims outlined in *Meet them where they're at* (and adapted from the *National Association of Youth Clubs* publication *Managing Detached Work. How and Why?*[54]) have been developed over time. However, we have continued to use them as a basis, and further adapted them to reflect a more symbiotic approach. These can easily be adapted for open youth club work.

Aims of Symbiotic Detached Work

1. To foster mutual relationships with young people who have few positive relationships and avenues for support and work alongside them to realise their full potential, recognising we will be changed in the process.

Detached youth work tends to focus on young people who tend to hang around on the streets and do so for a variety of reasons – many because of difficulties at home. For some young people the reasons may be more extreme than for others – having an abusive or alcoholic parent, for example. For others it may be a general lack of family relationships or just temporarily not being able to connect with, for example, their dad. There are other young people who just don't like the structure of youth clubs and others who are not into staying indoors watching TV or listening to music most of the time – they simply like to go out into the open air. Whatever the reason, these young people end up outdoors and this provides a great opportunity for youth workers to get to know young people in an unstructured environment and offer appropriate adult support and relationships.

2. To identify, discuss and challenge gaps in understanding between local community(ies) and young people so that new ways of being may unfold.

Much of the hassle young people are given occurs because of misrepresentation. Often young people who hang out on the street corner and are visible to the community are scapegoats for all the problems in the area. Part of a worker's role is often about challenging this type of stereotyping, dispelling these myths and helping both young people and the wider community gain a better understanding of each other.

3. To identify with young people their needs and interests and co-produce appropriate strategies for action, either by the detached team/young people, or with other agencies.

This is a general aim and a project may already be set up to facilitate the resolution of a particular need. It is important to consider the needs and interests of the young people themselves, as determined by them. Too often youth workers think they know what young people need or that the young people are deficient in some way because they are hanging out on the streets.

4. To enable young people to take more control over their lives, recognising the value and place of community.

Young people often feel that other people – parents, Social Services workers and/or teachers – are running their lives. They can be restricted in many ways, such as lack of transport, money or age. An important aspect of the worker's role is to empower young people to take responsibility for their own lives and choices.

5. To symbiotically evolve a new way of being community/church with young people.

As mentioned, in the ten years since *Meet them where they're at*, the aims of detached work (as set out by secular bodies) have developed significantly. One interesting thing to note is how much more they are in line with the notions of Symbiotic Youth Work. The latest stated aims from The Federation of Detached Youth Workers are:

- Be an agent of social change and social action, rather than social control;

- Respect the voluntary nature of the relationship between the worker and young person;

- Through negotiation and dialogue, challenge young people's attitudes and behaviour where they impact negatively on themselves and others;

- Support meaningful participation of young people in political decision making processes and ensure their voices are heard;

- Model such participatory values in all its interactions with young people;

- Support the progressive personal development of all young people towards self-advocacy through learning; [55]

Furthermore, it is important to point out that, in a youth work climate that is increasingly short term and targeted, these aims are open and will often require longer-term engagement.

These aims reflect what we were suggesting in the chapters Values-led Practice and The Genetics of Symbiotic Youth Work; that good youth work is rooted in inclusive principles that reflect much of Jesus' attitude to people and readily overlap with a professional youth work approach.

Detached work is a long-term approach to working with young people. It takes time to build real relationships. You sometimes think you've built a close relationship quickly with a young person on the street, but often young people have been let down before by adults and only time can cement the relationship. We would advocate the same long-term approach is needed in a Symbiotic Youth Work context nuanced by effective use of intentionality.

As previously stated, detached work is a highly versatile form of youth work and can happen in a number of settings. It is essentially going to where young people are, so you will find detached workers in all kinds of places, including cemeteries, street corners, parks, waste ground, the back of allotments, arcades, burger joints, youth pubs and bus stops. Detached workers are increasingly based in schools and this often happens as an extension of detached work in the community of which the school is a part.

Detached work can also work well in rural settings. The young people are not as anonymous as they are in towns and cities and may be known or related to a large part of the community. It can, therefore, be a bit of a challenge finding where they hang out: they tend to go where adults cannot see them, or they may be very mobile, as illustrated in the story at the beginning of this chapter. Different ways of initiating detached work need to be explored in rural areas, and different contact points need to be employed, such as travelling on the school bus or being around the bus shelter when young people gather for school or in the evening. Young people in rural communities face many of the same issues faced by young people in urban settings and so the aims of such work are fundamentally the same. However, in rural settings there is also a whole set of additional difficult issues to take account of: a lack of public transport, more limited employment opportunities, isolation, increased parental control due to the young people being dependent upon them for transport, visibility, and housing challenges to name but a few.

3

Safe practice

Young people's safety should be paramount in all forms of youth work and this should be especially considered when undertaking detached youth work in areas of social deprivation. Care and consideration needs to be given to the way you work. Here are some handy tips:

- Youth workers should NEVER do detached work on their own – going out in pairs is the minimum. Maximum numbers will depend on the number of young people that you are working with, but be sure not to have so many in the team that it is overwhelming for the young people.

- While on detached, workers should never split their team so as to leave one individual worker alone.

- Avoid any compromising or dangerous situations. You need to be 'streetwise' and look out for your fellow teammates. Don't walk into any dark alleyways or dark unlit spaces (for example, behind flats or under stairwells), even if you're with young people.

- A risk assessment should be completed before detached work commences. This should outline any dangerous places, known young people or members of the public who present risks and identify any other health risks or other needs.

- Have an agreement with a line manager or another youth worker to stay in touch whilst you are working:

  o Phone or text them before you leave to go out on detached. Give them a specific time that you expect to return.

  o Agree with them that if they do not receive a message from you an hour after the time you said you would return, they should try to contact you.

  o It might also be appropriate for them to contact other members of your family if you are due to return home after the session and don't appear to have returned.

  o If they are still unable to make contact with you, they might want to consider whether it is possible to drive around the area to see if they can spot you.

  o Finally, if contact is still not made, then the police should be called.

- Ensure you are properly equipped, with a fully charged phone (with credit) and some change. You may also like to carry a pen and paper, a first-aid kit and a camera along with any resources you think you might need; a football, Frisbee or pack of cards, for example. It is also sensible to make sure you have shared phone numbers amongst your team.

- Carry or wear a photo ID badge with your name, role, organisation and a contact number on it. This helps young people and members of the community appreciate that you're OK to be there!

- It is also sensible to make sure at least one worker has a first aid qualification and it is recommended that all workers undertake such training when possible.

- At the end of each session, it is a good idea to make a written record of what happened during the session, providing as much detail as possible. These session logs will act as a progression report, provide evidence of your work for supporters and funding bodies, and be used to develop further practice.[i]

During detached youth work, you may find yourself in situations where young people are involved in drugs, violence and criminal behaviour. Detached work is different to managing venue-based provision, as already noted: we do not, and cannot, enforce rules about the conduct of young people that we work with. On the street, young people essentially have the right to do as they wish and face the consequences if they transgress. As youth workers we must manage situations carefully. Team safety always comes first. In any situation where you feel at risk, or feel that someone else is at risk, you should take remedial action as necessary. This might mean leaving the area as a statement against the behaviour. It might mean giving a verbal warning or request. It might even mean contacting the police as a last resort or if you think their action is putting someone else in danger. This list of challenges and responses is by no means exhaustive and you should ensure you have proper policies and procedures in place before starting.

The street can be a place that promotes symbiosis: a sense of space and ownership that evolves and is struggled for; a place where the worker must negotiate and work creatively with opposing views; a place where versions of Symbiotic Youth Work can grow and evolve. What is clear is that detached work is a great context to start a process of Symbiotic Youth Work. It provides a great platform in terms of equality, its reliance on relationship and its approach to going to where young people are in order to develop mutual relationships. However, the detached context also means that, as Symbiotic Youth Work develops, it will often transition into other settings. Curry Church is a good example. The transition to these settings provides an opportunity to reinforce and develop mutual and co-operative approaches.

Having established what detached youth work is and how symbiosis works within it, we now begin to explore in detail the Nine-Stage Process; beginning with Stage 1, Observation.

3

---

[i] Various practice guidelines, session logs etc. are available through StreetSpace.

Chapter 10 – Stage 1: Observation

We could hear the voices from quite a way away as we had been wandering around the town looking for where young people hung out. On previous occasions we had seen a group of emo young people (young people who focus a lot on emotional feelings) quite regularly near the reservoir. However, they had disappeared over the past few weeks so our first thought was that this could be the same group, but now hanging around the back of the Co-op. As we walked through the alley we could still hear the voices but saw no visual signs. Then we heard a thud, and a young person appeared just around the corner. Suddenly it all made sense as we saw three or four others appear. They had been on the roof. Doing 'Parkour' (or free running) they said, as they wandered off.

Richard Passmore

Being effective explorers

A couple of years ago, as a family we went on a road trip across America from New York to San Francisco. We had never been to the United States before so it was all new to us and took a lot of planning and preparation. First we had to decide the route we were going to take. Easy you might think; but actually we changed our minds quite a few times as we factored in how far it was to drive from place to place and how many hours we would need to drive each day. Then we had to find accommodation at each of our stops that would fit the five of us in one room (to keep costs down). Then there were all the sights we were going to visit: Monument Valley, the Grand Canyon and the Gemini Giant, a 30ft spaceman (yes, really)! It took about a year to plan, but without all the preparation the trip wouldn't have gone so smoothly. The right balance of preparation and planning enabled us to know where we were travelling on particular days but gave us the freedom to wander off track when we wanted. We were able to book certain hotels with the intention of heading that way but we made sure we were able to cancel these bookings should we feel the need to go 'off piste'.

In order to be effective explorers in this new landscape, we will have had to make the necessary preparations beforehand. This will have involved some sort of community audit; finding out about the locality and things like ethnic diversity, geographical layout, employment levels and educational achievements. You should also have information about all the major players in the community: police, schools, health services and councillors for example. All of these preparations are discussed in more detail in Section 4.

Once that information has been gathered, it is time to move into the Observation Stage: the beginnings of the going out and doing the youth work bit! Observation is a chance for you to get the lay of the land. Even if the landscape is a familiar one that you think you know well, there may still be a few surprises, like young people appearing from your local Co-op roof! In this chapter we explore the skills you need to make the most of your observations and also how long-term research will benefit your youth work.

Acclimatisation and research

To assist you with this first stage, we are going to split 'Observation' into two tasks. Firstly *acclimatisation*: this means getting to know an area well and getting 'in-tune' with your environment. For example, you might be used to going about your local community during the day, but what does it look like in the evening or at night? What is it like in other parts of the locality where you don't often go? There are always things to learn and it is important for you to familiarise yourself with potentially new perspectives.

Secondly, *research*: not necessarily of the clipboard variety (though you may like to make notes when you get home to remind yourself), rather gathering information that will be useful to your on-going work. For example, make a note of where young people are hanging out, or look for signs that young people have been in that place. This might be some graffiti or a bin full of chip wrappers, maybe even litter.

There will always be a role for both acclimatisation and research in your work and it is important to keep this in mind as you move through the stages. By continually learning and gathering new information from the local community and from the young people you work with, the more effective a youth worker you will become – whatever the field of youth work you are involved in.

When 'observing', you may feel like David Attenborough waiting to turn to the camera and, in hushed tones, explain the indecipherable behaviour of the native young people! However, when we talk about observation we are not talking about a one-way process. Rather it is as much about the young people accepting you on their turf as it is about checking out where they are hanging out. It is a gradual process and not one to be rushed. That is why the term 'acclimatisation' might be more helpful, because it is not just about the youth worker being the observer, but also the worker being accepted and becoming accepted in the environment by the young people who have already laid claim to the physical space.

There are many ways in which observation can be undertaken and

3

often this depends on the resources available to the worker or project, the time frame of the project and what you hope to discover. There are benefits to being a youth worker who works in several different settings (for example, detached, schools and/or centre-based), as your face will get known more quickly and the young people will be used to seeing you around. If this is not the case though, there are still plenty of options for this stage to develop your profile. For example, try and get out when young people are about, such as at school finishing time or in the evening.

Rather than just aimlessly wandering about the area, try to be focussed. If the local upper school is near a supermarket, do your shopping just as the young people are leaving school. Go and get yourself some chips from the local chip shop in the evening. If you have a dog, walk it at those busy times for young people – you could even borrow a dog! When out and about, try to stay alert to any relevant activity.

As a team, or in small groups, get different people to feedback what they have found when out on observation: this will give different perspectives and also encourage the team to get involved at this observational level. You could even ask other people you know in the community where they have seen young people hanging out and when. In reality most people in the area will know places young people hang out, but you will often find a few tucked-away places.

Whichever methods you choose to use in observing, your safety and that of others in your team is paramount. Even though at this stage you are not actively engaging with young people, you need to make sure that you and the team are familiar with the policies and procedures of the project. As this may be the first time you or some of the team have been involved in youth work, it is important to make sure that adequate training and support is given by a more experienced, or professional, youth worker.

Here are some useful pointers to help your acclimatisation and research:

- Have a brief – this will make sure everyone knows what they are doing and why. It may also include what not to do. Anything that is agreed at this point should be recorded somewhere and kept on file with the rest of your notes.
- Have a designated route or routes – depending on the size of the group. Stick to the route.
- Write up what you have observed at the end of your session.
- Be specific regarding what you are looking for. You might have an aide memoir or checklist reminder to help you. For

example, you might be asking: How many young people? Where were they? What time was it when they were observed? Was there anything distinctive about that group of young people? What were the young people doing?

- Take different factors into consideration – for example, you might wish to consider the arrival and departure times of buses, cinema opening times, when pubs and shops open or close, what other adults are in the vicinity on a regular basis and what they are doing.

- Be inconspicuous – as mentioned earlier, a clipboard is probably not appropriate. Be subtle in your research, you want to blend in not stick out. Going as a group really helps, as you will probably remember different things which will give a better overall picture.

- Never stop observing! Goestchius and Tash[56] warn that once they focussed on working with young people in groups, they forgot to continue to observe and so at times they lost sight of how the community of young people and their group dynamics were changing.

Having delivered detached youth work sessions in a city centre over a four-year period, it became apparent through our observations that the young people's drinking habits were affected by the changing seasons, and the academic year. We observed that, as the schools went back after the summer and the nights drew in, larger groups would congregate in the parks, hiding in the unlit areas in order to drink alcohol away from prying eyes. In the summer, when it was light and they had more free time during the day, the attraction of drinking in the evenings was not so prevalent. This was backed up by conversations we had with them at a later date. These observations highlighted the need for us to continue observing and researching, so that we could be relevant and aware of the needs in that particular situation.

James Ballantyne

You will find that, after a while, your observation skills will become a valued and well-used tool in your youth work kit bag; one that will become well-developed and honed as you continue to use it in your youth work practice. Your observations can even provide a resource for conversation with groups as you progress through the remaining stages of the process.

Throughout the observation process, you will notice vital evidence that will be beneficial to your work. This will be quantitative evidence, such as the numbers of young people, groups and observed behaviours – for example you may see a reduction in the number of young people engaged in anti-social behaviour. Also there will be qualitative reflections, such as feelings, journeys and stories which will provide you with an emerging narrative of the life of the community you are working in.

You may at this stage be able to identify regular groups of young people that you hope to engage with in the future. For one team working in a city centre detached youth work project in Scotland, it became apparent after a period of observation that the city centre was a place young people would travel into, with different groups gathering on different nights or weeks. The young people would then leave from about 10.30pm. They also discovered the nightly flow of adults into and around the city centre, from buses and taxis to pubs, from pubs to restaurants and back again, and then onto nightclubs later on. Through conversations with the local police, they found out about shift patterns and numbers of police staff on duty. This one aspect of city life allowed the project to make predictions of routines, especially of adults, but also regarding the social dynamics of the groups of young people and their plans for splitting up and heading home just after 10pm. This meant that the team had a good idea of how much time they would have to engage with the young people when progressing onto the next stage of the process at a later date.

The nature of the context you are in will also determine the purposes of the young people you observe. It could be in a town or city centre, where you might find young people coming in from the suburbs and enjoying the local nightlife, or maybe young people on the run from the police. In a more suburban, rural or small community, you might find young people in a more specific place of interest like a skate park, outside shops or at a football pitch.

Other factors, such as lack of public transport, may also have influence. All of these are contributory factors to young people's behaviour and are what you are seeking to identify during any community profiling and observations. You may have a specific area you want to observe in mind, but be aware that hanging out in one area could be misconstrued, so assess this as necessary.

Fully appreciating the context

Understanding the context you are in is critical, especially the setting. A team in the coastal town of Hartlepool, for example, noticed that there were vast differences between the communities where young people congregated, and in the reasons why they did so. The long coast roads would be paradise for the boy-racers driving up and down to test their cars, but these roads had no natural gathering points. The young people would therefore stop in the towns for somewhere to join up, have a chat and generally check over each other's cars. For other less mobile groups, the spread-out town was problematic; so specific groups of young people stayed near to certain shops, or near the youth clubs.

In *The International guide on the methodology of street work throughout the world*, the street is described as a place where there is constant tension and fighting for possession of territory and survival. Maybe the harsh realities of street life in South America are far from the experiences we have here in Britain. Street work amongst the very poor in the slums of San Paulo is in stark contrast to rural England, for example. However, young people who use the street or other public spaces to hang out, do so for a variety of reasons. Importantly, out on the streets they are able to decide the nature of the environment, i.e. the activities they participate in, the social boundaries they embody, and the language they use. All these things help them to create a place where they feel most comfortable – as opposed to an environment that is constructed and moderated by adults, such as a youth centre, however informal and well-intentioned those places are.

For some young people, the street is a place to escape, a place to be with others, a place to gather or plan, a place to have power over others or to belong, a place to drink or eat and somewhere to be significant or important. There may be many reasons, but in our experience the street is rarely sought as a place where young people want to be alone. However, it is only after a period of truly experiencing the context that we can make any of these assertions with confidence. Until we start to engage with the young people, these are, at best, assumptions. Youth work, according to Sercombe's definition,[57] occurs in the young person's social context and so this is the place in which we are seeking to ultimately engage with them. This provides a good baseline for the beginning of Symbiotic Youth Work. It is respectful to them and in line with the values discussed previously. Also, it is good practice to begin by making an effort to understand something of that context, through acclimatisation and research.

> When I first went to the North East of England, one of the young people gave me a translation of the Hartlepool slang the young people used. He must have recognised that, as a relative southerner, I was going to struggle to decipher meaning from the local phrases. It takes time to make sense of local idiosyncrasies of language, especially as an outside

person getting acclimatised to a new culture.
James Ballantyne

Understanding others and deciphering codes and meaning in language is vital to becoming accepted in the context of young people. According to the theologian Kevin Vanhoozer,[58] it is not only mission, but also theology that we do with appropriateness in the cultures and contexts that we find ourselves. For this reason we must seek to understand, initially through observation, the cultures and contexts that we and the young people are in. We must consider what the signs and symbols are; the behaviours and actions; stories and narratives; and the language and meanings that shape the culture and community the young people are in.

Don't rush this Observation Stage. It may be at this starting point that you want to dive right in and get going as quickly as possible, but it takes time to make the right connections and engage with young people. It is invaluable in allowing you to see the bigger picture of the community of young people, both the individuals and groups within it. Theologically too, taking time to understand the context you are in will enable you to develop a contextually understood theology and create the right platform for mutuality. An understanding of the humility and nature of Jesus' incarnation may be helpful as an inspiration. We model, in our human way, a sense of becoming with the community around us, living with and amongst and spending time understanding, through day-to-day life, the markers of the community. Jesus' ministry was characterised by those who could not comprehend that he was local and real, but by being aware of the local customs he was able to re-attribute them to His new emerging Kingdom. This is not only borne out by his, "You have heard that it was said" phrases, but also by the fact that Jesus drew from customs and social dynamics in his parables and warnings (Matthew 5:27-43, Luke 15:1-10, Matthew 25:1-13). These had emphasis because they meant something to those listening. Part of the observations that are accomplished in the settings of youth work should also take into consideration the customs, rituals and spiritual dynamics that we are about to re-attribute, or encourage young people to reflect upon.

One of the key aspects of Goestchius and Tash's[59] work is that they realised that working with unattached young people in a detached setting not only meant working with the young people themselves, the community, and other services, but also that they were working with themselves (perhaps a forerunner of Symbiotic Youth Work). They recognised the extent of the effect that these observation sessions had on those who participated in them. Routines that are established at this Observation Stage will enable the on-going work to succeed, and this is down to the personal investment of the team. Therefore, it is imperative that those involved are well prepared, both before and after engaging in the youth work session. This may be as simple as asking the team if they are OK, or what their feelings are about the evening ahead and spending time afterwards, not only reviewing the observations, but also reflecting on how the session affected the feelings and expectations of those involved. It is as important to value each other as it is to value the young people you work with.

Symbiosis in Practice

- Be prepared;

- Acclimatise yourself to the new environment;

- Be proactive in your observations;

- Continue to observe throughout your work with young people; and

- Make a note of your observations, all the comings and goings, taking into consideration all the different factors (such as the time of year, time of day and weather) that influence what you see happening.

Adaptations for other types of youth work

In terms of an open youth club or drop-in, we would call this stage 'Observation and Development'. Whilst much of the guidance on understanding the context is still relevant, you also need to ensure you develop the drop-in on the right night, in the right venue and context. If you open in one location will you attract the young people you have observed who you are targeting? Will this location or venue put some young people off? Is it in a particular territory, or the wrong postcode? Applying the lessons discussed here will help you get the initial pitch right and then, when it comes to moving on, will give you the right language to find the best approach to how you will manage the space with young people.

3

Chapter 11 – Stage 2: Cold Contact – Initial Engagement

Cold Contact is that first moment when you make some connection with the young people you have been observing. It may be through just a cursory glance or some sign of recognition. After much observation you will be more familiar with your area and will have been able to identify where young people are hanging out in your community. Cold Contact is the stage that makes detached youth work unique in contrast to centre-based or building-based work. You go to the young people rather than the other way around and therefore you, as workers, are the ones who make the first contact. Regardless of how long you have been observing, it is only when you start a conversation with a young person that you start to understand, encourage and learn from the young people you meet.

> *A group of youth workers head out onto the exposed green area adjacent to the beach. With them, they carry a cool box that they fill with food, drink, bubbles, chalk and all sorts of goodies. The groups of young people they contact are often transient and they tend to see different young people each time they go out, but that doesn't mean that they don't get to engage with young people on a regular basis or that their presence isn't appreciated. "We came across a group of young people who were into heavy metal and who people were avoiding. When we said "hello", they engaged with us straight away wanting to know who we were and what we were doing out on a Friday night. It was amazing, because they were so happy that adults wanted to talk to them when normally people avoided them."*
> **Vicky Swift and Rebecca Bickerton, Coolbox**

Having years of experience in this type of work, we have pulled together our observations about how to do Cold Contact. This name might sound a bit intimidating, but it is simply exploring what to say, how to say it and what reactions you might get. Our reflections here are all grounded in our experiences and so we encourage you to read and digest this chapter whilst remembering that Cold Contact is simply about following the natural pattern of relationships that happen time and time again in our daily lives. When a young person moves to a new area they will rarely come right out and introduce themselves; they simply hang around on the edge for a while before joining in. It is much the same with detached Cold Contact and there is nothing to worry about.

3

Identifying groups

For many people, taking the first leap into the unknown of approaching and speaking to young people can be a daunting one – especially when it is adults approaching young people. If it helps reduce anxiety levels, you might like to think of it as 'encountering young people for the first time' instead of 'Cold Contact'. The crucial things to remember are to be yourself and that the thought of directly approaching young people is probably more nerve-racking than the actual reality of doing so!

Remember the tools you have packed in your kit bag and be ready to draw on those skills and experiences to help you. Being sure-footed is essential when forming relationships with young people in a public space. The challenge of not only encountering a group of unknown young people, but also engaging with them in meaningful conversation might not be something that you find entirely comfortable. However, it should not be something to get overly stressed about, or frustrated with if these first encounters don't go quite the way you expect them to – this is all part of the journey. Do not be daunted. Draw on your own life experiences. Youth workers in every setting (such as in a school, a mentoring project, or if a new young person comes along to the youth group) all encounter elements of Cold Contact – it's just a matter of breaking the ice in conversation with the young person. There is an element of 'coldness' about most of the starting points in all interpersonal relationships, not just those in youth work, yet the term 'Cold Contact' is one unique to detached work and has become the most unnerving aspect of it as a result. Here is what one detached youth work volunteer had to say about it.

> When we started to engage with young people on the streets, there was an excitement about it, almost nervousness, and fear of being attacked by the young people, [a sense of] not knowing what's going to happen or what we were going to be asked, or any knowledge of what each evening would be like.
> **Lynn Jack, Scotland**

The aims of your project will specify what type or groups of young people you will be looking to contact. You might, for example, live or work in a more rural setting where there is no youth club and so you might have a general engagement brief with young people. There may be other projects that have a specific brief for their work such as, for example, developing sporting activities or tackling issues such as drug abuse, gangs or underage drinking. In large urban settings you may find that young people tend to hang out in one particular area but that there are different young people each week. So whilst you might be positive about knowing the locations where young people are, the actual young people may change each time (as in the example given at the beginning of this chapter involving the young people into heavy metal music).

Let us assume for now that the young people follow a relatively regular pattern of behaviour. They hang out in the same place on a frequent basis, such as outside shops, parks or street areas. As explained earlier, you may be influenced by the criteria of your project and might, for example, be looking out for unemployed young people or those suspected of drinking alcohol. Unless the area you are working in is particularly large, it is best to make Cold Contact with all the groups of young people you have observed. It is important to contact young people when they are in that space, rather than when they are on the move. For example the young person might be heading for a bus whilst you try to engage them.

It is through this process of Cold Contact that you cast your net wide. Later, as you continue on your journey, you will filter down the number of groups you contact as you gauge their response and openness to you. This will be explained further shortly.

Approaching young people

Now we move on to the actual contacting. You have identified the groups, made your observations from a distance and now it's time to be more deliberate in walking towards the young people. If they have been watching you, just as you have been 'observing' them, then this will feel very deliberate, especially if all eyes swivel in your direction!

There is undoubtedly an element of vulnerability in the moment of approach, given that you make yourself open to the questions or inquisitive nature of the young people. There is also bravado in that you do not fear the power and control the young people may determinately have in that situation as you enter their space.

As you become more regular and familiar in a setting, you are going to be noticed more by the young people. They may call you over and want to find out what your motives and intentions are. For other young people it might appear as if they haven't even noticed you. In this situation it is up to you to make the first move.

It is worth mentioning the use of identification here. All StreetSpace workers and volunteers wear ID badges on lanyards around their necks when they go out. These have contact details on in case any queries are raised. These ID badges can also be a good way to introduce yourself and explain what it is you do when the opportunity arises. Some projects will have logos on t-shirts or

3

jackets to help identify workers. This can be useful on larger estates or city based work. Think about how to explain your intentions in a way that is jargon-free – especially of youth work or church language. You want to leave enough space so that the young people are inquisitive, but not totally bamboozled and/or patronised by the suggestion that you have somehow come to 'help' them.

As you start to walk towards a group of young people on their territory, it is worth considering what you think the young people might be thinking as you approach. Using our explorer analogy, as intrepid explorers in a strange land we may see this group of young people as a new tribe of people who dress and act differently to us. They see you. What might they be thinking? Will they wonder whom you work for? Are you the police? Are you there to have a go at them? Are you 'friend or foe'? It is worth pausing and reflecting upon these, and no doubt many other, questions that the young people might be contemplating. This will help your preparation and increase your understanding.

In that moment of approach, what you want to do is reassure the young people, respect them and put them at ease. Walk confidently, but not necessarily directly towards them which could be misconstrued as aggressive. Think about your exit points from the setting. Can you walk past them if they ignore you, for example? Also allow exit points for them, don't hem them in. For example, if they are sitting in a shelter, make sure you don't crowd the entrance, blocking their escape and perhaps only enter the shelter when invited.

How to read the situation

It is important to be able to gauge any given situation, as how it is going will affect how you then interact with the young people. Interaction might range from a simple nod and "alright" to going up and more formally introducing yourself. Here are some indicators that it might be appropriate to approach the young people:

- Positive eye contact;
- Accepting/affirming body language;
- A welcoming call/wave/sign; and/or
- A question from them, for example, "What are you doing here?"

It is a good idea to try and make eye contact with one of them as you approach and assess from their reaction as to whether to pursue your contact with them or not. Often the person you make eye contact with will be the person who you perceive is the leader of the group, but be careful here as assuming someone is the leader when someone else actually is can sometimes lead to intra-group conflict! We would still recommend being cautious at this stage, even if eye contact and open body language has been positively perceived. Psychologists tell us that it takes seven seconds to form an impression of someone and a further thirty minutes for that initial assessment to change. Therefore, the first seven seconds of engagement with the young person or group are vital: what you say once you have gone over will reveal what your attitude, values and intentions are. Take some time to think about what you will say and how you will say it.

Introducing yourself

We give the following examples to our young 'Zine volunteers when we train them to illustrate a 'good' and 'not so good' way of introducing yourself to a group.

No. 1: 'not so good'

> "Hi there, what's your name? Cold out isn't it? So do you hang round here a lot? Where do you live? I hear there are a lot of young people doing drugs round this way; you wouldn't know anything about that would you?! I'll be coming down here a lot, can I take your mobile number so I can phone you when I'll be around?"

No. 2: 'better'

> "Hi I'm Charlie, this is Bill, and we are detached youth workers. We are a bit like the youth workers down the youth centre, but we hang around on the streets with young people rather than being stuck in a building".

There are some very obvious shortcomings regarding the approach taken in 'No. 1' and a lot of what it includes is loaded with connotations. The second introduction is very straightforward and to the point. The young people might want to ask you some questions and look at your ID. You will probably want to follow up your introduction with a question – think about what you are asking. "How's your evening going?" is less threatening than "What are you up to?" which sounds like you might be accusing them of something! What you ask should reflect the offer of acceptance and relationship that you are seeking to give – it should show respect and a non-judgemental attitude. You could ask a question or talk about something happening in that moment, but do so in a positive way. For example, if the young people are hanging out near their cars, say something positive about their car. Don't tell them you have one the same; they won't want to know, at least not yet!

The top tip we can give you around the area of contact work and fostering a Symbiotic Youth Work approach is this: when you introduce yourself, explain to the young people that they do not have to chat and you are happy for them to wander off if they don't want you around. Often the more confident or loud group member will tell you to go and often in colourful language! If you turn to walk away, nine times out of ten you get invited back. This changes the power dynamic massively and you are then there at the group's invitation. In this early contact, be interested in them, though not in a sleazy way! Affirm something about them in that moment. You have information about them right in front of you – themselves. You could refer to their shoes, clothes, football team they support or music they are listening to in a positive and supportive way. All these things will make the moment easier. Keep it real, local and in the here and now. Notice them. First impressions are so important, so make them positive, accepting and non-confrontational. You are on their turf during their free time and now you have turned up – you are also now part of that space.

Now you wait. What is their response? Will they embrace your positive acceptance of them? They may wonder what it is you are getting out of this. This may lead them to ask if you are being paid to talk to them (it's a common question) or if you want something from them (perhaps to invite them to a church service) or something else. Many young people have not had somebody genuinely interested in them who accept them for who they are and approach them on an equal footing.

> We kind of went to walk past them and then, because they gave us eye contact and shouted something, we went towards them. It was a small group, about four or five I think (aged between 13 and 14) and they'd obviously been drinking. We asked how they were, and they wanted to know who we were and whether we would ring the police. On us saying we wouldn't, they chatted further. I am sure we ended up walking with them near to the cinema. I remember that one of the girls told us some really significant stuff about her home life and that she had been kicked out for the evening, so was drinking all night. For us it was a bit of a breakthrough – first group and all that. It gave us confidence in what we were doing there and how we could be helpful and significant in their lives.
> **James Ballantyne**

Be aware that your gift of friendship (bounded by good youth work practice) might receive a range of reactions: confrontation, boundary testing, suspicion and disbelief are just some of the possible occurrences. Be prepared for different reactions from each of the groups you contact. It is then your responsibility to try and read the motive behind each question and respond accordingly – don't forget to use the tools you have packed in your kit bag!

You also need to think carefully about your exit strategy – how are you going to leave the group? The skills you have learnt at the Observation Stage are all valuable when making judgement calls at the Cold Contact Stage. Acknowledging communication cues (verbal and non-verbal) is important in engaging in conversation and is also useful when deciding the right time to leave. It is important not to outstay the welcome extended to you by the young people.

Knowing when to leave them, or how to give them the option to decide when the encounter is over, should be considered, as should the need to leave well. In the same way that your approach and welcome to a group should be positive and easy, make sure that the ending of the conversation is too. Allow them to ask questions – they usually will. If your presence is causing problems within the group then apologise to them. If there is a natural gap in conversation and the group reverts inwards, then take that as your time to leave. Try to say goodbye when you go. Thank the young people for their time, or what they have said, and wish them a good rest of the evening/weekend. These are all simple things to say and things we would say to our friends or family as a matter of course. Doing this will ensure that the young people's last memory of you is a positive and respectful one. It is as important to leave the young people in a positive, affirming and non-judgemental way, as it is to initially engage them in that way. Not judging their next move is as important as not judging their first.

Adaptations for other types of youth work

In a youth club or drop-in setting, we use the same title of Initial Engagement, but there is very little 'cold' about the process. The reality of running a building will mean you have to know who is in the place in case of fire or emergencies. Therefore, you can use the registration processes to begin to get the names of young people and use this as the Initial Engagement process.

Chapter 12 – Stage 3: Cold Contact – Extended Contact

This second Cold Contact Stage is about developing your relationship with the young people following your initial contact with them. Timing when you do this is as critical as the first Cold Contact Stage.

Some young people may not want you to be around them. They may be planning their evening, or trying to find a quiet space away to drink alcohol, for example. You have to respect this as rushing to develop the relationship too quickly at this early stage could detrimentally impact the initial contact work you have undertaken. Take the positive from your first meeting – a nod, a quick "hi", or a deliberate turning of their body to acknowledge that you are there – but recognise now may not be the time (or the place) for further extending the conversation.

If you are fortunate, you may have encountered some of the young people in another setting. As previously noted, it can be advantageous to be involved in the community of the young people in different settings, as it may help if you already know some young people. Occasionally this can work against you if you are meeting young people in a more formal setting or in a context where the young people are not present voluntarily – they may consequently see you as an authority figure and this is not always helpful.

Building rapport

Ultimately, your focus is to build rapport with the group. This usually starts with just one or two young people within the group. Not all the group will talk to you in that first contact moment unless you are able to stay for a lengthy period of time. Take advantage of the opportunity if you are able to have a conversation with more than just the more vocal one or two young people. Getting positive rapport is the next step in gaining acceptance from the group and them accepting your presence in their space. However, getting accepted by the young people can take a while, as can building up a rapport with them. This may be affected by things such as their mistrust of adults, your infringement of their personal space, or if they or their friends don't like you.

With difficult or challenging groups, the temptation is to avoid them or not to engage with them. However, we would attempt to at least make some acknowledgement of them on each occasion – even if it is just a nod or a wave across the road. That way the group know that you haven't forgotten them. Should an occasion develop when they may need you or want to connect with you, at least some contact has been made that can be built upon – when they decide the time for this is right.

Beautifully unpredictable

The beauty of detached youth work is its unpredictable nature and rawness. Strangely, it provides the right environment for natural relationships to occur between supportive adults and young people. It is a new landscape that you both find yourselves in, a kind of third space of acceptance that is also unpredictable and potentially fragile. Detached youth work is not about the programmed events, structures, rules, regulations and timings that can govern more conventional models of youth work. The unpredictable nature of detached youth work means you will need to work very hard to do what is appropriate and reflect on each encounter as it happens. It makes it incredibly important to choose the right thing to say in that specific space and time as you do not know when you will next have such a moment – the group might move on or disband in the future, making each encounter highly valuable. The quality of relationships developed can be increased due both to the informality of detached work and also the respect and acceptance that is often shown by the young people increases as a result of us (as youth workers) making the first move towards them.

Symbiosis in Practice

- Use what you learnt in 'Observation' to locate groups of young people in your area;

- Be brave! Step out in confidence. Be deliberate in your approach to groups; and

- Acknowledge the young people, be it through a nod, an "alright", or a wave.

That initial conversation with a young person, that starting point on the journey, could not only represent the beginning of the offer of a significant positive relationship in the lives of the young people we meet, or space for education, but also a place for 'glimpses of God' to occur,[60] and the journey towards being 'church' to begin.

In Mark 10:46-52, Jesus asks the blind man Bartimaeus, "What do you want me to do for you?" It would have been easy for Jesus to just heal Bartimaeus, but he did not. If you look at the situation, there is Jesus on a journey, crowds clamouring, followers complaining about the delay to their journey and the blind man with fragile expectations. Jesus, much like when we are confronted by a noisy group of young people, takes that one person in need aside and asks him what he can do for him. In a moment of what could be described as 'Cold Contact', Jesus offers all his power, knowledge, mercy and grace wrapped up in that one question to Bartimaeus. When we think about how our work with young people mirrors that of Jesus and identify the Kingdom around us, we could do no less than to act, as Jesus would – showing respect, seeking to serve, being with and believing that Kingdom change is possible.

Adaptations for other types of youth work

Rapport Building is the term we would use to describe this stage in an open youth work venue – when you know the names from the register and need to build the relationships and find out what the young people are into. Here you can begin to introduce the young person to how the club works, explain how they might be involved and negotiate and discuss the club rules and resources. If you have a console or table tennis table these can act as a helpful sort of intermediate barrier to developing relationships – either by placing you beside the young person on the console or opposite them at the table tennis table. It gives you the chance to build the relationship slowly and slightly obliquely as you get alongside young people feeling their way in the youth club space.

3

Chapter 13 – Stage 4: Area Based Work

This afternoon I was on my way over to the local community centre, when I met someone and stopped for a chat. Along comes the leader of the 'DTO'* (a local gang of 18+ lads) on his bike. I looked up and smiled and said, "Hello". He nodded back, put his brakes on and, as calm as you like, said to me, "Do you smoke weed, love?" I replied, "No, it makes me mad!!" He pedalled off and I continued my conversation and then went on my way.

It struck me as I walked that I was pleased (and excited) he had said that to me, as it could indicate that I was trusted and accepted by the gang (at last!). Our project has been hoping for a 'way in' to engage with this group for ages – and I know that I am central to it coming to fruition.

I guess what I am trying to say is that, for me, it really is about the tiny, baby steps, just being who we are as people and being open to opportunities, no matter how they present themselves. That makes building real, lived relationships with local young people so exciting.

Heather Graham-Thomas, StreetSpace WSM

*Name of group changed for confidentiality

As we began this journey into the Land of Dragons, all we brought with us were (metaphorically!) the clothes on our backs, our wits and our well-packed kit bag. We had some clues about what might be up ahead, a few signposts, but knew the only way we would truly find out for ourselves was to go on the journey. As we have travelled through the stages of Observation and Cold Contact we have gradually begun to acclimatise to our surroundings and the young people we have encountered. Rather like the need for a good warm coat, hat and gloves in a cold place, we have started to understand more about the environment we find ourselves in and adapted accordingly. So now, not only do we carry with us our trusty kit bag, but also we are even better equipped to work more effectively in our area. Just as Heather found, you may be surprised by the impact your presence has had in the area and once you start to make those connections you can start to move that relationship forward. Heather's response and openness to the question she was asked showed the values of Symbiotic Youth Work in action. It was not a sense of shock or a judgement on smoking weed, but a feeling that a mutual space was being opened up. Heather is not going to smoke weed to enter that group and likewise turning it down will not be an issue with the group.

Having been involved in the intricacies of Cold Contact, making those first steps out on our journey, full of apprehension, excitement and nervous energy, now is the time to take a step back and look at the bigger picture, reflecting on how you are going to engage in detached youth work with young people. You've made those first tentative contacts and will start to see patterns in places where young people hang out, the rhythms or comings and goings of the young people through this period of acclimatisation.

The Area Based Work Stage is one that most seems to capture what detached youth work is all about. It is the critical and energising phase of the work, when you meet with young people and allow space to grow relationships with them on their turf. The energy and adrenaline of these moments fuels the work that you do. You will call upon the skills and experiences you have learnt through Observation and Cold Contact as new groups, new activities and new behaviours occur. This is especially relevant to those who intend to be working with young people in their community long-term.

Drawing on our explorer analogy, at this stage you are not just focussing on one tribe, but maintaining awareness of all the tribes that inhabit the land you are exploring. During the stages of Observation and Cold Contact you have identified the different groups in the area who have begun to accept you and whom you will be able to communicate with in some way. However, by continuing to focus on the whole area you are working in, you will be less likely to miss out on other significant moments with other groups.

Working in the area

There are advantages to working within the whole area, rather than just with one identified group of young people. These include:

- Raising your profile amongst many groups;
- Being inclusive – contacting groups of different ages, genders, ethnicity and background;
- Maintaining a more holistic picture of the life of young people within the community giving plenty of opportunity to find out what G-d is already doing in the community; and
- It also means that you do not become focussed on one particular group too soon, nor will they feel that you are exclusively theirs. This is especially relevant as young people often distinguish or separate themselves by subcultures – skaters or bikers, for example.

On one occasion when I was delivering detached work in a suburban area, two different groups who we had been working

3

with came together. Whilst we were chatting with one of them later in the evening, they questioned why we had spent time with each of them; not because the groups were enemies, more that they had different interests/subcultures. On that occasion I could explain that as a detached youth worker I was available to all the young people in the community, regardless of their own designated subculture, likes or activities. It was a moment that helped us to understand our inclusive role, unfolding a new community, and to be aware of all the young people in the area. They also realised that neither of the groups owned us, even if they wanted to.

James Ballantyne

Continuing Area-Based Work is key to retaining a sense of inclusivity. It also avoids dependency on the young people's part, setting the right tone for symbiotic practice. In light of this, if you go on detached within the community on more than one evening each week, it might be worth considering the frequency with which you visit different groups/places. Perhaps choose not to visit one place one week, or visit at different times, especially if you have spent a lot of time in one place on previous occasions.

This may be difficult if there are obvious areas in your community where young people hang out – like at the local skate park or in a car park. You can, however, pass through a place: make your acknowledgements but move on rather than stay. Be respectful that this is their space and sometimes they will want it for themselves. However, we can learn from that power-changing moment in the Emmaus road story: when Jesus looked as if he was moving on, the disciples begged him to stay with them (Luke 24:28-29). When you are giving space or being transient through a place and the young people call you over, at that moment you have received permission to be with them, so make the most of the privilege.

Sometimes it's easy to get caught up in the moment. Perhaps if you have had a particularly positive meeting with a group of young people, there can be the desire to continue this next time you see that group. Be aware though that the young people may feel differently and that lots of different factors could affect the mood or situation in such a way that means it is not appropriate to just pick up where you left off. It is important you check your perceptions when engaging young people; do they want to speak to you again? Be patient. Treat every encounter as a new one, reading the situation and doing what is appropriate in the moment.

The questions the young people ask, their body language and group dynamic will differ from session to session and place to place. It is important to be aware of this. Just because something has happened one session, doesn't mean it will the next. Even within the space of a session, the young people's behaviour can alter depending on whom they are with and what they are doing. For example, interrupting a group when they are in the middle of drinking alcohol might not be the most appropriate moment for a lengthy conversation, even if they give you a nodded acknowledgement! However, by being active in your area other opportunities might arise when you can have that lengthy conversation, perhaps when they are hanging out in a bus shelter or on a bench and are up for a chat.

Area-Based Work, as opposed to specific targeted work, gives you space to work within the whole area and with a variety of groups of young people. This allows you the freedom to not just stay with one or two groups for a whole session, but to consider the whole area you are working in. By casting your net wide and moving from place to place within the area, you will show the young people that you have not targeted them specifically and that you have a broader mandate. Therefore, as the relationships develop, they do so voluntarily and often at a pace set by the young people. Because you move across the whole area, the nature of your role as a youth worker is reinforced. It is small issues like this that will help you develop the right balance between mutuality and appropriate adult relationships with young people within a Symbiotic Youth Work paradigm.

One of the objectives of symbiotic detached work is to be accepted by the young people's subculture in their space. Area Based Work gives you the opportunity to engage with and be accepted by a number of different groups from different parts of the community you are working in. You will discover the paths to acceptance will be different with each of the groups you encounter. They will differ in their acceptance of you; some may barrage you with questions to try and test you, others will tell you exaggerated stories or achievements, some might ignore your questions or give closed answers. Some young people will be considerate with one group of friends and rude when with another. They might show their acceptance through the offering of food, such as chips, a handshake or a positive comment. Be wary of these gifts though: their meaning could be misconstrued and may indicate that they want to possess or own you. It is important to keep the approach mutual and co-operative, rather than simply being a service provider.

Do not take rejection too personally. It is an expected part of detached work. Developing relationships takes time. Young people may not readily accept or appreciate what you are offering,

3

especially if they consider this service irrelevant to them at this time. The unpredictable nature of young people's behaviour is part of the challenge and joy of meeting with young people in their different contexts. Take all of what they give to you through conversation as a challenge to overcome. Consider how you can react appropriately with that long-term goal in mind. There is no failure in realising that the right thing to do in a particular instance is to walk away, but be persistent in your endeavours – acceptance takes time.

Having positive conversations

Conversations are key to good Symbiotic Youth Work. Not only do conversations allow for the mutual flow of information, the building of rapport and a chance to get to know one another, they are also places where informal education can take place.

Conversations within the detached environment are multifaceted. Sometimes conversations can be brief and one-sided without much response from the young people. At other times you will have in-depth conversations. The constituent parts of a conversation are important, each playing an important role in shaping that 'moment' and the education that takes place within that engagement between yourself and the young people.

In their book *Informal Education: Conversation, Democracy and Learning* Jeffs and Smith[61] discuss conversation as a process that is co-operative and reciprocal. This fuels symbiotic practice. Conversations can involve the intuitive, instinctive reactions of people, and also the agreement on a particular subject matter. Therefore, it is worth considering the effect of the context on how conversation develops in Area Based Work: it takes place within the young people's 'space', and in the public domain.

You may think engaging in conversations with young people on their turf, as it were, may be challenging because you are in their space. However, your presence may create intrigue and therefore stimulate questions from the young people, especially as they try to get to grips with who you are and what you are doing. Your role may appear ambiguous in contrast to someone with a defined role, such as a teacher or police officer. Given that your role may be unclear and that you have come to speak to them, you may find you immediately receive a level of acceptance, or superficial respect, from the outset. The young people may also be more at ease because this is their territory and so conversation may flow more easily.

You will be involved in lots of conversation in detached work – with the young people and also within the team of workers. It is

3

important to remember conversation is reciprocal and therefore it may involve a level of openness on your part. You will also need to be skilled in questioning (though not in a Spanish Inquisition type of way) and listening, being able to affirm and respect the young person throughout.

Being able to gauge the situation and draw on the right tools to aid effective conversation is vital. There are situations where asking pertinent questions, framed in the right language and style, will encourage lengthy personal conversations. Consequently, you will be able to support a young person through any issues they are facing. At other times, for example in a large group, when conversation is mostly banter, these types of questions and questioning are not appropriate and their significance is lost. Sometimes this is difficult as you may want to engage with the young people on a more meaningful level, but as Heather Smith suggests,[62] it is important to consider that the chitchat and banter has as much intrinsic value as a more lengthy conversation. There is a skill in being able to facilitate and recognise the meanings within the banter and not just in the obvious content involved in personal disclosure. Heather Smith goes on to say that this kind of banter often provides the oil for the wheels of a relationship.[63] In Area Based Work, there is a lot of what might seem to be just banter going on, but these types of conversations are spaces of exchange, of acceptance and of challenge, and key platforms from which symbiosis can emerge.

Helping to construct a conversation

Out on detached, conversation seems to be the only tool or activity to hand; there is no table tennis table or organised activity to fall back on. In some ways you are exposed and so it is crucial that you are aware of how conversations are constructed.

Each conversation is made up of opening questions or statements, questions, listening, divergence and tangents, cues or clues in sentences for developing a subject further, humour, stories, shared experience, tone, reflection, changes of subject, use of words and meanings, power, control and silence (when appropriate silence can be a good thing, sometimes things don't need to be said). As well as thinking about how to open a conversation, which can set the tone for the whole session, consider the end also. You want to make a good impression throughout your time with the young people.

The power dynamic of the situation suggests that, where possible, the young people should decide upon the content of the conversation, particularly at this early stage. As the relationship with young people develops, you are more able to mutually develop the content of discussion, but here it is about creating the right base as you get to know the young people and they get to know you. When you are given the opportunity to pose an introductory statement or question, reflect upon something within the immediate context. For example, you can converse about their evening plans, the music they are listening to or an activity they are talking about. Even if you don't have a clue what they are talking about, just encourage them to reflect on what it was they liked or disliked. With Area Group Work, you are in it for the long haul, so be patient. Topics of conversation will arise naturally without you having to steer or mould them to your own agenda. Your very presence may give rise to conversation. When a police car goes by, they might vocalise their thoughts towards police. You then have an opportunity to reflect with them on their attitudes.

Going back to the conversation on the road from Jerusalem to Emmaus (Luke 24:13-19), Jesus joined the disciples as they travelled, he listened to their conversation and then asked about what they were discussing. When they referred to "all the things" in Jerusalem, Jesus asks "What things?" This is an example of effective conversation. Jesus joined and listened to what was being discussed and asked them to explain further without the need to insert new information. Later he was able to re-appropriate what occurred in light of information he knew (vs. 25-27), but during the initial conversation he gained their trust by allowing space for them to talk and share their story. In detached work we should seek to do the same. Jesus did not dispute the disciples' view of events, belittle them or condescend, even though he had lived through the preceding chaos in Jerusalem. How we give value to the young people's lived experiences, perceptions and feelings is fundamental in our respect of them and offers opportunities to explore and discuss, whilst recognising the power dynamics of the territory we are working in.

There can be a desire to shape the conversation in some way and to employ methods that introduce an agenda or topic for conversation – perhaps something we think is important for the young people to be discussing. If we do this, it will seem like the topic is not negotiated through the conversation and that we have an external agenda. In these situations you may want to reflect on how you felt when someone encroached on your territory and set the conversational agenda. Launching into a conversation about under-age drinking may not be appropriate if none of the young people are drinking at that time. It might be viewed as judgemental or confrontational. You may not know the personal circumstances of the young person/people, so asking about things like family, school or employment matters could touch on sensitive issues. Being skilled in the art of conversation and recognising the complexities of it in the detached youth work context will help you be mindful of what you talk about in the young people's space.

Being out with their mates in the evening may be their chance to escape and unwind from their day. Asking how school was may seem like an innocent question to you; but it might be loaded and parental-sounding to the young person. Also, bear in mind what questions you ask individuals in a group setting and what information that young person may or may not want to disclose to the rest of the group. For example, they may love school or hate it: both can be a reason for not wanting to discuss the subject. (However, if you work in a school, this can be a hard topic to avoid.)

You should find that conversation flows easily out of any given situation. If the context you find yourself in shapes the content of the conversation, then in some way the young people have co-operated in the choice of conversation. The following phrases can help in furthering the conversation in a respectful way: "Would you mind telling me more about _____", or "Would you be OK if I ask a question about _____". This negotiates their permission to deepen the conversation.

Rather than introducing subjects like school, work or college, for example, wait for the young people to bring these subjects up and use the natural opportunity to talk about them. Given the instinctive nature of these early conversations, invariably you make mistakes. If this happens, it is important to rectify the situation as quickly as possible in a sincere way. Apologise if you have overstepped the mark or asked the wrong question, even if you felt you didn't. They may appreciate the humility, but be careful not to overdo it, and recognise that in a mutual relationship you need to be who you are as well.

As a well-meaning, but naïve worker I initiated a conversation with a group of young people on the subject of football, which quickly led to a heated conflict within a small group about football teams. Prior to us arriving, the young people were chatty and happy, and so it was important to de-escalate the situation, apologise for the conflict caused and leave. Sometimes as workers we need to recognise that topics of conversation we bring up may have unseen consequences and that we need to remedy the situation.

James Ballantyne

If your intentions are both in the community and long-term, then overcoming mistakes with some humility will help you gain acceptance and respect, even more so as young people will talk about you amongst themselves.

Multi-purpose conversations

Through using conversation, you can also educate. This may happen when a young person is discussing a situation that has happened involving friends, school, family or something that occurred during the evening. You can use this opportunity to help them reflect, to consider their actions and others' feelings, and encourage them to look at alternatives or offer coping strategies for feelings, situations or worries. In some circumstances it can be useful to encourage the young person to visualise or articulate their next steps. For example, you could ask them what they will do when they finish their exams or complete a work placement. Ask them to think about how they can achieve their goals and if they would like your support in achieving them. Using these types of non-directive, brief, pro-active techniques in conversations and encouraging young people to process a situation is relatively easy. The skill is being able to facilitate this within a detached youth work context. This is where the benefit of being in a team, or pair, becomes apparent: one worker can continue to engage with the wider group allowing the other(s) to give individual advice or guidance should it be required.

After gaining acceptance from the young person or group, you can enable them to reflect on situations that are troubling them; perhaps their concerns with formal establishments such as school, social work or health professions. In our experience, it is becoming more apparent that young people have a mistrust of these sorts of organisations. Even their own GPs can be viewed with suspicion, which often arises through misinterpretation or an actual negative experience that they, a friend or relative has had. It is only within the space of a conversation that we can reveal these realities and provide strategies, or empower the young people, to resolve specific issues.

It may be worth noting this could also be the experience young people have of church. Recently, negative experiences shared with one worker included the perception that they had been brainwashed at Christian events: being trapped in basement rooms as part of Sunday school, or being bribed with entertainment to then watch a video about Jesus. It may not just be public negative perceptions of church or Christians, but also personal ones. Explore these real experiences, feelings and perceptions and don't be threatened or upset by them. This could be an appropriate opportunity to explore 'church', 'faith' or 'spirituality', or even apologise on behalf of others. This is especially important if you communicate your links to the Christian faith community.

There is no coincidence that the events of the Emmaus road occur where they do (Luke 24:35). At the time, Jerusalem represented a traumatic and confusing place for the two disciples. With rumours of stolen bodies, miracle resurrections and forsaken hope, it is no wonder they decided to leave the epicentre of confusion. It is on that road that they encounter Jesus. It is on that road that Jesus encounters them.

The road is a neutral, public place that leads the disciples towards safety and home. When considering the road to Emmaus, we can begin to think about the young person sitting on the wall, or in the shelter, and how – like Jesus meeting the disciples on the road – we are there with them in that moment of reflection as they react to the events of their day. Sometimes in Area Based Work you might meet those on spiritual, emotional, or cognitive journeys to and from conflict or confusion. You are there to bring light and space to their journey. The only way you can do this is by being there, in that place. Whilst there are skills and tools that can be used in conversation, there are no magic formulas. Each moment is different, shaped by many variables. You have to rely on your sensitivity to react to these appropriately. There are not always positive effects, but sometimes it is just important that you be there.

Symbiosis in Practice

3

- Continue to use what you have learnt through Observation and Cold Contact;

- You are working in the whole area, not just with one group; this helps raise your profile with other groups, promotes inclusivity and helps you see the whole picture;

- Keep it fresh; continue to work in the whole area, perhaps visiting groups on different days/times;

- Be prepared to briefly acknowledge groups, respect their space;

- If they invite you, take advantage of that invitation;

- Work in the now; gauge what is happening with the young people in the now and don't expect it to be the same as what's gone before;

- Acceptance takes time;
- Develop good conversation and listening skills; and
- Sometimes it is just about being there.

Adaptations for other types of youth work

In the context of open club work, we discuss this stage as Integration, and again conversation is central. There are clear opportunities, games, or resources within a club setting that help develop conversation. However, like in a detached setting, it is important the young people do not see you simply as a service provider, but that you set the tone for mutuality well. It can be easy to raise unrealistic expectations with questions like: "what would you like to see in the club?" Instead consider how to begin to use conversation to help the young people understand the context of the club, the resources available and the possibilities.

3

Chapter 14 – Stage 5: Peer Group Work

This is the stage where you purposefully hang out with large groups of young people that share a common interest. Peer Group Work is a slightly strange stage in that it may or may not exist according to the context you are in.

> In Chard, we had developed a project around the local skate park with a core group of young people and were building up to hosting a community day to celebrate the installation of new skate park equipment. The skate park was already getting a lot of use and we had identified that it had become a gathering point for young people in the area. On an average night there were now between thirty and forty young people using the space with anything up to sixty-five across the course of an evening. This meant we needed to increase the time we spent in this location to engage all the young people hanging out. It was clear there was a group of about thirty young people who could be defined as a peer group – this group were all committed to the space and either skating, BMX riding, blading or using a scooter. The core group we had worked with had raised over eighty thousand pounds to redevelop the park, so wanted the celebration day to go with a bang. It was decided to utilise the peer group to deliver postcard adverts to every house in the town. When we arrived with the boxes of cards, there were around thirty five young people present aged between ten and twenty-three. The older ones put themselves in charge of groups and we managed to deliver about one thousand postcards in one night. Most people in the town got one through their door, but a few were creatively spread out! When the event came round, it was easily the best attended we had seen in the town.
>
> **Richard Passmore**

Sustaining emerging relationships

Our ability to build and sustain appropriate, effective and valuable relationships with young people is at the heart of youth work practice... The relationships that we develop are significantly affected by the circumstances in which they take place and by the knowledge, skills and attitudes brought to these circumstances by those that are relating to each other.[64]

It is inevitable you will begin to forge relationships with the young people you contact as you get to know each other and begin to have deeper conversations. Being able to manage these relationships is important for both you and the young people.

Creating space for these relationships to develop from Cold Contact into on-going, appropriate youth work relationships is a significant factor, and we will consider how this sits alongside the symbiotic issues in Stage 7: Risky Small Group Work. These relationships and issues will differ according to your context, whether your work is detached or centre-based, for example. This is not to say that either approach to youth work is more effective than the other, but the distinctive DNA of detached work will mean that emerging relationships will take on different characteristics.

Huw Blacker[65] explores how the nature and quality of relationships are influenced by the circumstances in which they develop. As you increase your presence in the area, you will begin to see groups emerge. You may have started to connect with these groups and noted any shared interests that maintain their cohesion, such as alcohol use, football and lifestyle (for example being a Goth, skating or friendship dynamics). The activities these groups engage in and the fluidity of these groups will dictate how easy it is for you to engage with them. For example, if the young people group together to drink alcohol, its availability and accessibility will affect the dynamic of the group structure. Similarly, if the young people are actively engaged in, for example, playing football or skating, these activities themselves can be a barrier to conversation. In this situation, conversations often happen on the side-lines or in the in-between times. Having spent time in the area, you will begin to assess the regularity of these groups and their shared interests.

Fontaine et al[66] explore the context of the street as a space that is fought over, but also a space that young people choose to be in for a variety of reasons. When working in other areas, such as undertaking detached work in a school setting, it is worth noting that there is a limit as to where young people can 'choose' to hang out within this space, as opposed to in the public spaces they may occupy in their own time.

Groups congregate, whereas seeing individuals out and about is usually happenstance or occurs because they are 'in transit' to or from somewhere. In the majority of cases, young people in groups have made a conscious choice regarding size and membership, often glued together by shared interest or intention. Each individual will have their own reason for being in this group, and this group as a whole, may inhabit the space differently to any other group.

The dynamic of the group in their chosen territory will have special benefits and significance to the young people. The group setting on the street may be a place where the young people find acceptance, belonging and respect: even though you may not personally agree with their behaviour or values. It is a social experience for them (though conversely they are often labelled 'anti-social'), a space where they find safety and security, confidence and a place to experience transition. Robert Putnam[67] argues for the overall benefits of belonging to a social group to the health of the individual. Therefore, there may also be social and emotional benefits for the young people seeking out friendships in groups. This is applicable to informal groups as well as organised groups such as youth clubs or uniformed organisations. As you meet with the young people in larger groups, consider the benefits of the group association that they may be feeling and look for ways to encourage this. Socialising and community are as significant for young people as they are for adults. These social, or shared interest groups are important to the young people, even if they are temporary in nature (such as during the school holidays, when larger peer groups maybe more noticeable).

One of the advantages of being committed to and working in the area long-term (years as opposed to months) is that you will be able to observe the changes in the dynamics of the group. For example, young people sometimes move on to other interests, as they grow older. The young men down at the skate park sometimes shift into hanging out in their cars once they have passed their driving tests. A group of young people who drink alcohol may only do so for a short phase, which may progress into parties, pubs and clubs as they get older. Understanding the transitional nature of groups is key when thinking about opportunities for you to interact with them. Also your setting – rural, urban, suburban, or coastal – will affect the dynamics. The only way to do this is to spend a considerable amount of time in the area.

You may also come across long-established groups that have set boundaries, rules, hierarchy, shared stories and experiences, some of which you will have picked up on during your observations. You therefore approach this type of group as not only a collective of individuals, but also the collective 'substance' of them as a group, along with their narratives and perhaps some of the bravado that might accompany this.

Being purposeful

Once you have identified groups that meet regularly and who respond positively to you (as outlined in the previous chapter), you can begin to pursue a more purposeful and mutual relationship with them both as groups and as individuals within those groups. There are several indicators that the evolving relationship is moving beyond just positive interaction and conversation towards something more symbiotic. These include: their welcoming of you into their space; the disclosure of more personal information about themselves; a relaxed approach to your interaction; recommending you to their friends; and being more honest with you. They might also demonstrate positive or protective behaviours towards you. On some occasions, individuals within the group may actively seek you out, outside of the boundaries of the group.[i] This reinforces the idea that the group are accepting of your presence and role. This acceptance may be a calculated risk for the young people to take in allowing you to be present in their group at that time.

If you endeavour to interact with the young people in a considered and respectful manner, in accordance with good youth work and Christian values, it is natural that you will start to move into a reciprocal relationship with them. Not only will they accept you and the gift of relationship you are offering, but they will want to spend more time with you. Different groups will respond differently. Some may accept you quite quickly, whilst others may be wary and more of a challenge. With respect and perseverance this can be overcome.

Your involvement with larger groups thus far may feel somewhat superficial (though not insignificant), and can seem to lack that deeper, more detailed relationship. It can sometimes feel like your progression into the Peer Group Stage is a slow one. You may have started to understand the dynamics of the group – who are the potential group leaders, the energetic ones, those on the edges – but still you may find that the immediate situation prevents you from being able to get an 'in'. Nevertheless, the continuing 'drip-drip' of your regular presence should allow you to move the relationship on through conversation or collective action, such as fundraising to put lights in at the skate park, or by offering personal or individual support. We need to recognise, in the shifting landscape of post-modernity, young people, groups and community relationships are more fluid than ever before.

There may be opportunities whilst you are with the group for breaking down barriers, such as providing first aid (adhering to your policies and procedures) or being alongside them if the group is challenged by an adult. An opportunity to show allegiance to the young people in a direct way like this can give you some added kudos, but don't try to manufacture these situations to win favour. It might be tempting to somehow move the group along and force the development of the group work quickly in your desire to work more

---

[i] We would not put off a young person who may want to speak to us alone, but you need to ensure that you adhere to any safeguarding policies and procedures set in place by your project by, for example, making sure you are seen by another member of the team and that you are not alone with a young person.

intensely with the few. But in the long term this could do more harm than good. You have to allow the group to dictate the pace of the relationship.

Depending on the context you are working in, there may be some crossover between this Peer Group Stage and the Basic Small Group Work Stage. If, for example, you identify small groups of young people in your area (of perhaps six people or less) you might move straight to undertaking Basic Small Group Work. Also the sizes of individual groups may fluctuate depending on the time of year. For example, in the summer months when the weather is better, or during the holidays, you may find there are larger groups of young people hanging around or none at all. Sometimes you will find a young person in the setting who is able to give their perspective about other groups of young people in a given area – this is usually an older young man or young woman. They might be proud of giving you a tour.

> On one occasion at a skate park, one of the guys walked us around the area and told us who was who, giving the colloquial names for the small groups that hung around the facility; from the tinies (scooters), slicks (bladers) and SBS ('Skateboard Slags¹ – the girls that hung around and admired the boys).
> **James Ballantyne**

It is these moments of acceptance, of identifying a key person, which should allow for an easier transition or 'in' with the group. This place or person may represent "someone who promotes peace..." (Luke 10:6) as explored earlier when Jesus sent out the seventy-two, also telling them to stay in one place and spend time with the people there. On other occasions, Jesus takes advantage of the opportunities that arise from his initial contacts, such as staying in Peter's mother-in-law's house for example (Mark 1:29-33) and building on family links (John 1:40-42). Yet on other occasions it is the locality that is a hindrance for Jesus (Mark 6:1-5). Your interaction with these groups of young people may influence other groups in the community, or help in the development of your group work. It is important to make a good impression with these young people as, particularly in small town communities, acceptance by other groups may be at stake. How they react to you on future occasions will also be indicative of whether it is appropriate to be around at that time or not.

---

¹ This terminology might seem derogatory and go against our values, so you can challenge the language carefully at this stage. Then, in our progression to move symbiotically with the young people, there may come a point in one of the later stages to explore their values and challenge them more where appropriate.

Encountering these large groups in public spaces is both daunting and a bit frustrating. You may find you want to further the conversations you are having with a particular group, or individuals within a group, but sometimes the conversations are superficial at best, or the young people may barely acknowledge you. You need to balance this with the fact that you are in the young people's space and that your acceptance within the framework of your fledgling friendship is dependent on them. It is important to manage your own expectations, whilst recognising that developing relationships in such a large group will take time. Each time the group acknowledges you or responds in conversation is a step forward, but don't take their ignoring you to be a step backwards; it may just be it is not right on that particular occasion.

On the streets, a planned conversational type of approach (such as you might employ in a mentoring session) wouldn't work, as you need to allow the relationship to naturally develop. There needs to be some freedom or 'going with the flow'. Like the analogy of tacking, it is about immersing yourself in the young people's culture and seeing where this leads. You cannot apply rules or form to the way you interact with the young people. However, be encouraged! If a young person chooses to respond to you voluntarily then there is a level of acceptance and trust in that moment.

Symbiosis in Practice

- Groups often form around common interests;

- Spending time in your area or community will help you identify these groups in terms of regularity, interests and shared stories;

- Look out for the signs of acceptance from the group that might indicate your transition into a deeper level of engagement;

- Your continued and regular presence is never 'time wasted', even though you may sometimes get frustrated with the rate at which some of the relationships with the groups of young people are progressing; and

- Don't rush it!

Adaptations for other types of youth work

This stage is where the detached work context and the drop in stages begin to converge. The equivalent of this stage is where you try to develop the whole club mentality and maybe now know the different groups of young people inhabiting the different spaces of the venue. They may not seem much like a peer group as they spread out across a venue but you could easily see a sense of Peer Group Stage emerge as they feel committed to the club, accept your and their place in the space and begin to identify with the context as their space. You may also have the added advantage of being able to build on this sense of peer identity through large-scale group games and activities, developing the shared space through arts and setting the rules and developing the context through together identifying, for example, a group name or logo design.

3

Chapter 15 – Stage 6: Basic Small Group Work

The team had read that Pip Wilson used the question, "If you could make one wish, what would that wish be?" as a good way to open up conversation. Although they agreed this was a good conversation starter, at this stage in their contact with the young people, to ask that question in such a stark manner would be a non-starter. So, inspired by the story of Aladdin and his lamp granting wishes to people, they bought a magic lamp from a fancy dress shop and took that out with them instead.

The lamp was a good tool to get the conversation flowing; telling their wish or writing it down and putting it in the lamp involved the young people. It was a great tool for the team to use to move the relationships on.

"The most interesting results were those (young people) that aspired to something ordinary. They were profound in their blandness. Once they had got beyond the superficial, they began on wishes that were more real (but never aspirational)... Things like, 'I wish my bike worked properly'. 'I wish we could go on holiday, we never go on holiday'. 'I wish I could keep my bedroom tidy, then I could use it'. 'I wish we could go to the woods'. We have begun to weave into our work some of these wishes (like camping in the woods), but others have simply given us a window of understanding into the lives of the young people.

A 'tidy garden' was the most bizarre and perhaps the most precious wish – it's easy to read too much into it, but I think this wish says something about how the person feels and how they think other people see them: perhaps about wanting safe places to play, perhaps about being proud. It's a fascinating insight."

John Wheatley, StreetSpace WSM

This was a creative way of helping the team to move on their relationship with the young people. It was not the lamp itself that was important, that was just the tool, rather the conversations they had because of it.

Encouraging intensity

Basic Small Group Work develops when the larger, diverse, sporadic group of young people filters down into smaller groups who become more comfortable in your presence. These smaller groups begin to trust you more with their stories and personal situations. They may seek your advice regarding situations or issues they are facing that

3

are both immediate and more long-term. Basic Small Group Work is identified through its more intense regularity and presence. The exchange of more personal stories and significantly reciprocal conversations increases as you also share stories or information with the young people that encourage or enable reflection. Basic Small Group Work begins to occur when there is co-operation and negotiation of group tasks or activities during the time you are with the young people.

> *One evening on detached whilst we were driving around with hot chocolate prepared in our car boot, we screeched to a halt when we saw three young people we knew. We were invited to walk with them: what a privilege. They were so happy to have us stay with them for over an hour. They needed to go to meet friends (for larger rizzlers!) later on and when we began to say 'bye' they asked why we weren't coming too! So we did go, had more great conversations, met more young people and were even able to give some health advice to someone who it transpired (following a visit to A&E the next day) needed some treatment for a heart condition! A good night on detached.*

Dan Potter, Thornbury StreetSpace

Having become accepted, and almost expected, within the young people's context as a youth worker, there is a natural progression of some smaller groups of young people to seek you out. This could be those you have identified as leaders, or those on the edges of the group. It is as these smaller groups begin to forge a relationship with you within the context of the larger peer group that the relationships can deepen. It is important to note this change in the dynamics between you and the young people. How these feelings are expressed is down to the young person's personality and that of the group. They could be expressed through, for example, the young people welcoming you to the group; the young people knowing your name; you knowing all their names; them gathering round you; and others joining you when you are talking to one young person.

It is important to be aware of this development and change of intensity and prepare yourself for how emotionally connected you may become to these small groups. As you have sought to contact the group over a period of time, had lengthy conversations, maybe offered them support and started to establish an appropriate friendship with them, the relationship has become more purposeful. As you pursue these voluntary symbiotic relationships with the young people, recognise the affect they have on you can also be significant as you become involved in their lives, problems, worries, hopes and dreams. These are not relationships that have been

3

enforced or coerced: these are fluid, natural and symbiotic relationships between you and the young people. What emerges is still an appropriate relationship with young people that is redefining professionalism within a symbiotic context, rather than the distanced context that Ian Sparks highlighted in the chapter on Values-Led Practice.

Supporting the symbiosis

At the beginnings of this relationship, you need to recognise its fragility. As a voluntary relationship, it could end at any moment. Therefore, this is a good time to look at mechanisms you could implement to help further the symbiosis with the young people. This might involve taking them into a different setting; negotiating a new activity together – perhaps an extension of an activity they already participate in, such as a trip to a different skate park; a football match; or finding somewhere you can meet the young people over the winter months. These might be relatively easy to suggest and resource and can be a way of helping the group bond outside of their usual setting. Eating together, for example, is the great leveller and doing something simple like going with a group to get some chips will help this process.

Once these small groups have been identified, take time to consider how the group functions and what the group needs are. What are their expectations of you? For example, if there is a small group of girls in a larger group of young men, they might speak to you about the pressures they face within relationships created in the group, or others might want extra support if they are having issues at school.

As you engage with the group on a mutually inclusive basis you will find they present you with many types of issues and injustices – such as lack of facilities, cuts to youth services, or age related discrimination. As youth worker, your role will be to see how you can encourage and empower the young people in relation to the things you have discussed. Providing and offering your support in these areas will strengthen the relationship further. However vocal the young people are about the issues, they may not have a strong group dynamic (this may be apparent to you). Some of these small groups may have only developed recently and your role will be to encourage and develop the life of the group in a positive way. Whilst the context of the group is still the street, it is a natural group formed by them and your role is to facilitate and advise in a truly empowering symbiotic way, rather than dictate to or lead the group.

It is important to note here that you should not promise too much at this point. It is easy to slip into wanting to motivate or encourage the young people and get carried away. For example, in our local project the young people wanted to develop the local skate park and put in some new equipment. We started by raising funds to first extend the footprint of the skate park, then we raised money to install lights so they could use the park in the evening and finally we put in a large bid to install new equipment. By doing it in this way it kept the young people's interest, set realistic goals and prepared the young people for the process as each stage of project got bigger. As already mentioned, we then ran a special opening community day, which was so successful that we have been hosting it annually ever since.

As the groups of young people you meet on detached have formed naturally, the bond between them may be sufficiently strong that they may not only be peers, but also friends too. As a group, they have shared street experiences, or interests, and have bonded through these. Also, the young people will be connecting with one another electronically and through the use of social media, using Facebook, text messaging, or Twitter.

Changing dynamics

You need to recognise that your introduction to the group will affect the established group of young people. Be aware of your impact on them and how your presence as an adult will change the dynamic of the group. Reflect on your own behaviour within the group. Be a neutral presence without power, or take a negotiating role with the group as they begin to accept you amongst them. Respect them. Try not to influence the existing habitus. Instead listen and take the role of guide and facilitator when and if necessary – your presence in and of itself will help something new begin to unfold. Use language to reinforce your desire to take this sort of role within the group. Defer to the natural leaders of the group to make decisions. By using language in this way you create the space for them to take the lead, not you. For example, if they ask open ended questions you could say, "It's your life, it's up to you what you do". If you are talking about jobs don't say, "You could become a farmer", but rather ask, "What are you interested in?" to draw out their thoughts. Try to avoid using closed questions where the young people can only answer "yes" or "no", such as, "Have you ever thought about becoming a farmer?"

As you interact more with the group you will notice the roles the different young people take within the group. Some will seek to control and dominate (a frequent behavioural trait in the 'survival' mentality needed on the streets) and they will do this in a variety of ways, such as through having access to a vehicle, alcohol, drugs or

3

money. Others may be 'go-to people', the ones to approach when you need something sorted, or if you need to use a mobile phone. In larger groups there may be those who are more on the edge and are quieter. In the small group context though, this occurrence is less prevalent. You may witness a certain amount of manipulation going on, or highly complex dynamics that somehow hold the group together. Within some communities, families and their reputations hold sway within a group. As an accepted member of the group, getting to grips with the way the group functions is important as you seek to empower and facilitate in collaboration with them. Seek to channel the young people's natural abilities and talents to creative or productive use.

You will learn more about their stories, the reasons they are there, their needs, what's going on in their lives that has encouraged them onto the streets and also the hopes and desires they have for their community (according to *their* values). As you listen and learn, you will soon realise the complexity of their situations. This may go some way to explain some of their outward behaviour that is sometimes employed to mask more significant issues in their lives.

At this point your engagement with the group is contained within it. Conversation is primarily at the discretion of the young people and what you hear is what they choose to disclose to you and their friends. It is during this small group work that your creative and facilitating skills as a youth worker come to the fore. In a detached context, these skills will need to be honed and sharpened ready to use as the opportunities arise. This may be through storytelling, dreaming dreams with the young people, empowering them through conversation, negotiating the space to advise and formulate plans of action. You might choose to use technologies or materials to assist you in the street context, such as using a portable tablet computer, mobile phone, notepad or chalk to write and plan. Take into consideration the context and community you are working in to decide what to use with the young people – or even whether to, as they can sometimes be a distraction. Some young people will have access to the Internet on their phones so they may choose to use these instead.

Being involved in this way with a group over an extended period of time will enable you to help them achieve or accomplish something outside of themselves which wouldn't have been possible before your engagement with them. However, it is not something that will have required taking any risks at this stage. (Risk is something we will explore shortly, in Chapter 17). In the time you have been with them, you could have encouraged them and helped facilitate change in their lives, helped them develop coping strategies and given them the confidence to do something new within the strengthened relationship you have with the group.

Pausing for reflection

You may be beginning to see that Basic Small Group Work takes time: not only the process of getting to this stage, but also the process of group work itself. Identifying a group and creating a platform of trust, where the young people come to accept you and your guidance, and negotiating the needs and issues they consider you trustworthy enough to pursue with them all takes time – not to mention the step-by-step process of working towards realising a goal with them – whether this be going on a trip, a personal change such as giving up smoking, or building a shelter in your local park. Your role with the young people at this stage is to enable the process that initiates these things and negotiate with them when and where these are to take place.

The challenge at this point is retaining the open quality of your approach to the young people's needs and aspirations, especially if your work has a focus to meet a particular agenda or tackle a specific issue. Often neither 'church' nor 'issue/agenda' based work will be successful if this dominates the relationships being established. For example, telling young people they have to give up drinking to meet certain targets is less likely to succeed compared with giving them something to work towards in their lives, families and communities that encourages self-esteem, positive group work and decision-making – which in the long term may help reduce unhealthy behaviours, such as alcohol misuse. Likewise, having a long-term view of creating space for church to happen instead of telling them to go to church (in relation to the 'bridge into church' model discussed earlier in Chapter 3) is more likely to be effective. It is for this reason that detached work is of most value when viewed as a long-term endeavour centred on the needs and interests of the young people, rather than on the agenda of the work or organisation. It involves time, creativity and patience.

Working amongst the young people, you will begin to reflect on the different signs, codes and values of the group, some of which will differ from your own and from those of the organisation or community you represent. This will cause ethical challenges that you as a team can work through with the young people. The expectations of the young people may differ to your own. For example, the consumption of alcohol may be a means for the young people to feel as if they belong; yet you may think that it is caused by boredom, whilst others in the community might consider such

3

consumption rebellious and anti-social. A similar disparity of perspectives might exist regarding matters such as the completion of schoolwork, being employed, or dropping litter.

Many of the decisions made by the group will stem from the value-base endemic within the group. You will need to reflect upon how these values have been created and what your response to them is (in the light of your relationship with the group), whilst also balancing this out with the expectations of the organisation you work for, or the local community. If you turn to look in your kit bag here, you may have need of a magnifying glass. Whereas before we were looking at the new land through binoculars, trying to see things far away more closely, here we are helping the young people to take a closer look at things. We are giving them a glimpse of the values you have as a worker, or member of the community, and asking them to reflect on their own values in the light of these. In some ways, this is offering an opportunity for us to magnify the values of community, worker and young person in unison.

There will be opportunities to challenge the views the community have of the young people through, for example, policy-making, activities and events. Through running the community event in our local project in Chard, we were able to create an inclusive space for the young people to interact with the surrounding community. The young people demonstrated their skating, biking and blading skills, whilst at the same time we offered a bouncy castle, food and activities that appealed to the wider community. We had great feedback from the community: "It was a great family day for us and the sun had its hat on all day", "This was a fab event please can you do it again – my son loved it!"

Whatever the situation, it is likely that, when working in a small group, you will face some ethical dilemmas. It is important that there are people within the team's support structures who understand this and what you are trying to do in the long term. Engaging with young people in such a symbiotic way does not mean you become one of them. Therefore, you need to consider the boundaries that are in place to protect you and the young people. You should act appropriately in each situation, adhering to your organisation's policies and procedures. For example, if you have to ring an ambulance against their wishes in order to save a young person's life, then you must do so. But is it necessary to contact the police every time a young person uses racist language or is drinking alcohol in public? However, if racist language is used in your presence, and this goes against your own values, will you choose to counteract this with a positive comment or simply ignore it? What might be better for the long-term relationship with the young people? In all likelihood, it will come down to how you challenge such views: each situation is different, as is each group and individual. Chapter 6 was entitled Values-Led Practice because these values must be brought to the fore in an appropriate way.

Church is described by Rodney Clapp as a 'community of friends'.[68] As we discussed earlier, we see church starts where Jesus is with others, so we believe church is at the very beginnings of our encounter with the young people. At this stage we see this new community of church is beginning to unfold as we create connections with the young people who consider themselves our friends. Clapp goes on to describe how church is a place where stories, tragedies and celebrations are shared. As you interact with the groups of young people you will begin to understand the shared stories, celebrations and tragedies that bind them together and see the gap between church and community close. In our locality in Chard, a young man suddenly died after an asthma attack. Next there was a murder and then a car death all in quick succession, which all greatly affected the young people we were working with. Out of these tragedies grew the idea of having a remembrance gathering down at the local skate park.

The communication of shared experiences for the early disciples would have been equally important as they began to form the new church in Acts. As they watched, heard and participated in the creation of the new Kingdom, they would have reflected on what was going on around them (Acts 1:13-14, 2:42-47). Similarly, you and the young people will encounter shared experiences, stories and memories that bind not only them as a group, but also you to them.

Bonding may also come about through celebrating personal successes or achievements, parties or anniversaries the young people share. As an outsider to the group it is important that you are able to not only validate their experiences, but also encourage their stories and the emotions that shape the group.

Symbiosis in Practice

- Identify the smaller groups and begin to move the relationships on;

- As you symbiotically connect with the young people, recognise the affect they, and the relationship you have established, will have on you;

- Don't raise unrealistic expectations;

- Respect the make-up of the group and take a neutral role within it;

- Use language to create space;

- Begin to work out how the group functions. What roles do the young people take within the group?

- Hone your creative and facilitating skills!

- Their values may differ from yours and the community. Think about which reaction to these ethical dilemmas will be most beneficial in the long term; and

- See the benefits of shared experiences.

Adaptations for other types of youth work

Basic Small Group Work is a stage in this process most youth workers will be comfortable with, given that a lot of engagement with young people occurs within group settings (in schools, clubs or churches). Here we see the full convergence between detached work and centre-based provision. Developing Basic Small Group Work in a detached setting requires different approaches in respect of the role of the worker; but Basic Small Group Work in both settings needs to be facilitated with patience and endurance in order to react to the chaos of group work in the open setting. Basic Small Group Work is a place where the magic of natural relationships and conversations occur, where something new becomes more of a reality.

3

Chapter 16 – Stage 7: Risky Small Group Work

We had known the group for a long time and several young people had helped with the redevelopment of the skate park. It was now one of the best skate parks in the area and certainly a great asset to a small town. So when the group suggested they do a further extension, it seemed a very self-centred idea and conversation. To challenge this, I told them in no uncertain terms how selfish I thought this was and that they should think about doing something for others. This sparked a conversation about Africa, which led to the idea of doing something with a local charity that supported work in Romania. I had no idea at this point that it would end up with a group of young people going over to build a community pharmacy in a village in rural Romania.

Richard Passmore

What do we mean by 'Risky'?

Risky Small Group Work is the moment when the young people take deliberate risks proposed by you. To clarify, **facilitating a culture of risk-taking does not mean that you expose the young people to any form of dangerous or unethical risk**, such as un-safe youth work practice, drug taking or violence. The 'risks' that we are proposing here are those which seek to challenge the young people's actions, values or behaviours. The "in no uncertain terms" phrase used which prompted the young people to consider doing something for others was actually, "You bunch of selfish gits!" Making that statement risked the relationships built so far by directly challenging them on an issue – you might even say it was a justice issue.

As previously discussed, you may have already been witness to the familiar risk-taking behaviour that young people often engage in, such as alcohol or drug use. From our perspective, we may view this type of self-destructive behaviour as a product of their conditioning, or of thrill-seeking, and not actions to be encouraged. The 'risk' we advocate is that of positively challenging this behaviour.

There is also a personal risk involved – the risk to the relationship you have built up with the young people as you begin to test these relationships by challenging, for example, the derogatory way they talk about someone, their sexist behaviour, how they litter the area and their views on and use of violence. This proposed risk is grounded not only within the established group work of which you are part, but also within the supportive relationship you have forged with the young people. Within the bonds of this established

3

relationship you will feel ready to suggest an action, or pose a challenging question, that is deliberately provocative in a personal or social way and requires a change in behaviour or attitude of the young person. By choosing to take this challenge and risk with the young person (or group) you inevitably assume a slight position of power or control over them, so be mindful of this. It could be that the risk factor is in the assertion of power, rather than in the challenge itself.

When a young person responds to a challenge to do something new, or is willing to move out of their chosen context (park, street, or car park, for example), it indicates a measurement of the trust they have invested in you: trust in relation to how much they want to spend time with you, or how much they value your advice in dealing with issues they are facing. When we are talking about risk, we do not necessarily mean something big or dramatic. It may be the offer of support to an individual, or something like undertaking an activity together that may involve travel (if the young people don't normally venture further afield than their own community). Though these issues may not seem particularly challenging, they do require the small group of young people to trust you. This may come at a personal cost to them, especially if other people in their lives have previously let them down, as demonstrated in the story below.

> "Will you mentor me?" – the words of a sixteen year old girl who just wants to be listened to, cared for and shown love ... a girl with anger issues and a history of eating disorders and alcohol abuse ... a girl who feels loved when being abused by boys who only want her for one thing ... a girl who slowly, surely and more confidently is starting to see that she doesn't have to stay that way ..."
> **Lisa Hayes, Hope37**

Remember, these moments of risk are best entered into when you have well-established relationships with the young people rather than at a contacting stage. Throughout the detached work process, you will have been dabbling with risk (taking the risk of being on the streets, the risk of rejection, of them talking to you) and now you are challenging the young people to journey with you in a collaborative risk. As you have been working with the young people and perhaps had some positive experiences and enjoyed spending time with them, you may have become a bit comfortable. Now is the time for the edginess to return, to provoke challenge and help the group and individuals to grow.

Options for challenge include asking direct questions, using stories or scenarios to aid their thinking and/or challenging their reactions, perceptions or assumptions by giving them new experiences. It is most likely that challenge will emerge in conversation, when it feels appropriate to suggest the risk. Up until now, discussions around these issues may have been broad in scope, or ignored by you. As your relationships with the young people strengthen, you now have the opportunity to challenge them or offer support. Only you can assess or judge when it is appropriate to start taking risks and what tactics to employ with the small group you are working with.

Small step-by-step risks

Like all the Stages so far, the risks can be taken step-by-step. At the start of this process we described the setting as if we were strangers in an alien landscape, noting the many tribes that inhabited the space. To further this analogy, when contacting a tribe in a new land for the first time it is important to ensure that they know your presence isn't a threatening one and that you respect their boundaries. You might have brought them gifts from your own land and withdrawn respectfully until you were invited into their space. The same is true of risk-taking with young people: it is achieved through the gradual process of taking small risks, which lead to larger ones as we gauge their reactions and test the boundaries of the relationships.

Take alcohol misuse as an example. If the young people you encounter are drinking harmful amounts of alcohol, it is an obvious step to address this issue. Through your contact with this group you may have talked about alcohol in a broad sense, but you might take a risk by taking a more direct approach. Your motivations here are that you want to offer your support as they work through this issue and related concerns. Being direct might mean asking the young person about their history of alcohol use (or that of their family) and of their dependency on it. You might start a conversation with: "Do you remember your first drink, or the first time you got drunk? Why did you feel it was what you wanted to do?" Being direct in this way with a young person, especially in a group situation (and especially if they are male), could be particularly risky if alcohol use is considered the norm within the culture in which you are working. The risk here is posing a deliberately direct question. It may result in further conversations, making the risk one worth taking. However, if you take too great a risk, such as making the offer of one-to-one support, it might be unhelpful to the group and their expectations of you. Such an offer might be made further down the line once you have dug a bit deeper, got below the bravado and are able to more clearly see that this type of support would be valuable to the young person.

3

Taking risks with young people is usually a step-by-step process. The encouragement of this risk-taking may be a pre-planned one worked out with your fellow team members. As a team, being aware of the possible consequences of taking such risks, even though you won't necessarily be able to guess correctly the young people's reaction, will at least mean you feel more prepared. You can reassess the risk possibilities on each occasion that you encounter the small group. Each risk taken can develop further trust and acceptance of you. This increases confidence in you and creates the climate in which it is possible for you to facilitate greater risks with the young people and so on. The developing symbiotic relationship that you have with the young people will lead to shared experiences, moments of challenge, trust and also personal vulnerability or increased community. Therefore, you can start to incorporate the new adventure of risk into every encounter with the young people.

These risks do not need to be significantly large, or particularly direct, on all occasions. The risks could be something as simple as asking the young people to pick up other people's litter in their vicinity; developing plans for the local community; exploring conversationally themes such as hope, death, life or poverty; or it could be creating spaces to consider prayer, identity, sharing, or personal values. You could take some food out with you and encourage an impromptu picnic, card game, or ceremony of some sort linked to a birthday, local custom or national celebration (Bonfire Night or Christmas, for example). It could also be taking the group out of their familiar surroundings to a different space, such as a building, going for a walk, or anywhere that differs from the norm. These are only suggestions and you will have your own ideas as you get to know the young people you work with. We would encourage you to always have an element of risk about your work when the young people are at this development stage.

It is during this Stage that we would implement M&Ms. Participation in M&Ms is done on an invitational basis through the team. The young people invited are those we have established relationships with and we let them know what being part of M&Ms will involve. During M&Ms the young people take part in various consultations on a range of issues such as, town planning or the cuts to the youth service, which we then feedback to the necessary organisations. This allows the young people to actively participate in consultation processes on a range of issues. We also use this space to plan trips, residentials, and share stories (such as the Flow stories) with them. It was within this context of growing risk that the story at the start of this chapter took place – the perceived selfishness of the young people was challenged, which led to the Romanian trip.

Risks and relationships

Being able to take such risks with the young people is only possible because of the relationship you have forged with them over a period of time. At a personal level, the risk may be yours as your values are challenged by young people and the symbiotic alignment with the young people begins. Each time there is a response to risk; the boundaries and possibilities of the relationship are widened; especially if the response to the risk is a positive one. Encourage the young people to reflect on their responses and feelings towards the challenges and risks you have engaged in.

It could be said that embarking on a symbiotic relationship with the young people is a risk in itself. Risk involves relationship and relationships in youth work provide the platform for real change. The benefits of a long, considered and participative relationship, which has been invested in and cultivated as you have travelled through the stages, are that risks and trust are possible. Other approaches, which do not take such a considered and time-invested approach, where change is required of the young people, lead to the young person not trusting the challenge being proposed, or the person who is proposing it.

The symbiotic relationship you have with the group engenders a feeling within the group that you are in this with them. It indicates that you support them and this is important for the co-creation of habitus. This is not about failure or glorified success (which are both possible), but about something new emerging. The important thing is the trust you have earned from the young people, that they are willing to take these risks with you and that throughout the process your support has illustrated to them the respect and care you have for them as individuals in that moment of risk.

Take, for example, when Jesus invites Peter to get out of the boat and walk on water towards him (Matthew 14:22-31). The foundations of Peter's trust were cemented in his relationship and knowledge of Jesus and so he was willing and courageous enough to take the risk of walking across the water to meet him. Although Jesus was there to pick him up, all wet and embarrassed when fear overcame him, he failed alone: none of the other disciples took the risk to get out of the boat. When you challenge the young people to take a risk, don't set the bar too high. Allowing them to fail or be embarrassed in front of their friends and peers (aka Peter) might not be appropriate. Give opportunities where they can achieve in order to reinforce their trust in you. Support them in the risks you are asking them to take. Ultimately be surprised and encouraged by positive reactions, but realise that if they do not wish to partake in the risk you may be moving too fast for them, or it might not be appropriate in that moment. If the unfolding community is growing, then you will together be able to cope with particular failures, to help build togetherness and support to move on.

This risk-taking that encourages the young people to engage in certain activities could be seen as a way of preparing them for the next stage – the 'risky' Exploration of Spirituality. Risk-taking in itself can be deemed a valuable attribute to a young person's faith and spirituality. These moments of risk awaken the young person to new possibilities of expanding their boundaries and getting out of their comfort zones as they acknowledge the relationship they have with you.

The nature of the relationships you have created with the young people, from the context of the streets, to the group, to further group work, is underpinned by voluntary participation. At any point the young people may decide to no longer participate, engage or converse with you. By working on the streets, this choice is presented to and worked out with the young people. This symbiosis begins to mirror an incarnational way of doing youth work and also the nature of the creator/creature relationship between God and Humanity. When created, we were given free will to choose to be in relationship with God. God did not enforce or dictate this relationship. In this way Humanity could make up its own mind whether to believe, listen and respect God or not. The act of incarnation, the sending of Jesus to earth, represents a dramatic risk by God of intervening in the living history of the earth, and becoming amongst his creation. Jesus is God's definitive word and act:[69] by being with Humanity in physical form Jesus was able to present to them ways and means of a new created relationship with God.

As people (such as the crowds or the disciples) built up their relationship with Jesus through moments of following, healing or understanding, Jesus seemed to test the resolve of these relationships through risk-taking or by stretching the boundaries: sending the seventy-two into the villages, feeding the five thousand, inviting Peter to walk on water and the questions that he asked of them, such as, "Who do the crowds say I am?" (Luke 9:18). For those on the receiving end of a miracle, there was an element of personal faith/risk-taking, such as pouring out the water at the wedding banquet (John 2:6-7) or dropping nets into the water (Luke 5:4-5). Jesus also responds to the spontaneous risk-taking of others, such as the woman at the well (John 4), the woman who touched his cloak (Luke 8:45-50) or Bartimaeus who shouted for mercy (Mark 10:46-52).

It was because Jesus was there, amongst them, encountering people in their contexts, that he could give them opportunities for relationship and also the space to take risks. These moments of risk shaped the relationships Jesus created around him, yet those relationships were also voluntary, as not everyone followed or accepted him. Steve Griffiths[70] makes the distinction between 'chronos-time' (a measureable period) and 'kairos-time' (to do with the moment), suggesting that Jesus was not dependent on chronos-time. Whilst Griffiths recognises the importance of Jesus spending time with the twelve disciples, he shows the importance of seizing the kairos moments as they arise. You need not wait until this stage of Risky Small Group Work before you seize these moments. As we have stated, spirituality is embedded throughout the whole process and we recognise that if church starts where Jesus is with others, it starts with Cold Contact.

Those who followed Jesus did so on the understanding that it would involve culturally-subversive risk taking and trust in the person who was setting the risks. To the young people, the growing and unfolding community emerging may itself be a culturally-subversive process that differs significantly to the norm of their context. At the same time, the quality of community already shared by young people with their friends may have a lot to teach the newly unfolding co-developing community/church. Therefore, whilst Griffiths is right in recognising the weakness of a youth ministry that fails to seize the moment, suggesting that it should be rooted in kairos-time may not be the whole picture. For Symbiotic Youth Work, we feel a more balanced approach between the two is needed if a new church/community/way of being together is to emerge. Jesus' chronos time with the disciples was vital for sustaining and rooting the newly unfolding habitus emerging among them. This enabled them to make the most of the kairos moments with others and to use these stories as landmarks that could continue to resource and inform them as they continued their journey in the new land. The additional and intentional risks we may take at this stage (as well as the other kairos moments that have happened from day one) can be the future landmarks to the new community.

After Jesus, the mantle of relationship-building and risk-taking rested on the disciples who shared this with others (Acts 8:26-40). In a similar way, by going into the context of young people on the streets or in the club, you give them the opportunity to take a risk by building a symbiotic relationship with you.

Symbiosis in Practice

- The 'risk' we are talking about here does not put young people at risk and is not dangerous or unethical; it is rather a challenge to actions, values or behaviours;

- There is a personal risk to the relationships you have developed as you test them;

- Risk = Trust;

- Challenge can include asking direct questions or by challenging the young people and ensuring a repetition of challenge;

- It is a step-by-step process; and

- The risks take place in chronos-time (your relationships with the young people that have been developed over time) and kairos-time (in the moment).

3

Chapter 17 – Stage 8: Exploring Spirituality

The first evening we went out for a meal at McDonalds, I said to Daniel that as part of the meal we would have a time of sharing and say grace before we had the meal. We first found some tables where we could all sit together, which is quite tricky in McDonalds, but we managed to pull some tables together. We got our food and all sat down. We then went around the group each person sharing one thing that was on their mind. Then Daniel said it was time to say grace, but before we could start one of the young people said, "We always hold hands to say grace", so we all held hands. There was lots of joking about how soft each other's hands were and stuff, but we said grace and that was that. Anyway, the next night we thought we would go out for a proper meal so we went to a Pizza Hut in a very white middle class place with this group of black kids in their hoodies and bandanas. They were noisy, being young people, and we were getting some looks from other diners. As before we had our time of sharing and then we said grace and without having to say anything the young people automatically held hands to say grace. It was one of those amazing moments where it had become part of what we did without us having to prompt anything.

Stu Thomson, Knights Youth Centre

When we talk about Exploring Spirituality at this stage, we do not suggest that 'spirituality' will not have been woven into your previous encounters with the young people as, "...spiritual development is not simply one theme or idea within a programme, curriculum or set of outcomes; it is the context in which everything else takes place"[71] Rather we are identifying that this Stage in the symbiotic relationship is a natural point to explore spirituality in more depth, as you would any other relevant issue.

As discussed earlier 'spirituality' as a term can be quite difficult to define, and its meaning can be interpreted in a variety of ways. This is no less true for the young people you work with; even the word 'spirituality' may have little or no meaning to them. Nigel Pimlott[72] writes about spirituality:

Some have suggested that we are talking about an awareness that there is more to life than meets the eye, an understanding that life is full of things that inspire awe and wonder, a rationale that incorporates paradoxes, the unexplained, and mysteries. Others have reflected upon the sense that life is a complex journey weaved by understanding and grappling with the issues relating to comprehending ourselves and others, the

environment that we live in and the unquantifiable 'out there'
subjects of God, the non-material and the transcendent.

Spirituality and stories

One way we have explored spirituality with young people in our local context is through the use of story, primarily the Flow stories (some of which are included in this book). This approach has also been used by other StreetSpace projects experimenting with other stories that may connect with their groups.

Story can be found throughout history as a way to pass on knowledge, to illustrate, interpret, warn and inspire. The Bible is full of stories, with Jesus using stories in the form of parables throughout his ministry, making the inaccessible accessible. In the same way stories can help spirituality become more accessible to the young people you work with.

There is much discussion about how young people of generation 'Y' (those born in the 1980s and 90s) connect with spirituality and the concept of the happy midi-narrative.

> *The assumption embedded in this worldview is that the meaningful happy Ideal is achievable. If it turns out that it is not then the disparity between expectation and reality can be very difficult to deal with. Once happiness is seen as a possibility it becomes an individual's responsibility to achieve it, and if it is not realized it is seen as nobody's fault but their own.*[73]

It is not a very encouraging outlook according to some and, to give a very broad, sweeping generalisation of this view, it is that today's generation of young people are at best neutral on the subject of spirituality as they make their way in the world in pursuit of happiness. However, we see in the image of the Trinity that relationship plays an important role in spirituality, God in relationship with Himself. We have already highlighted some of Griffiths' concerns about locating relational youth work in chronos time and here we need to further question the idea that youth work starts and stops with individual relationships. The Trinity demonstrates the communal nature of G-d and as such the un-understandable nature of this. Therefore we need to move beyond seeing relational youth work as a tool to help a single young person connect with God and instead see the inherently communal and ecclesiological nature of relationships. This requires recognising that Symbiotic Youth Work moves us beyond the individual and is about allowing space for the young people to connect with their spiritual selves within the context of your trusted and trusting reciprocal

3

relationship, which itself is something deeply spiritual.

As you spend time with the young people, you will begin to uncover and discover themes of spirituality within their relationships and lifestyle (for example. connecting into the young people's expressions of 'Flow'). It could also be defined by their identity, state of mental health, reactions, emotions, hopes, dreams, fears and aspirations for the future and how they understand things like the meaning of life, science and creation. These themes allow you to explore 'other' with the young people you serve and the relational communal role is key. This is not to say the individual gets swallowed up by the communal (in the way that can happen in some large-scale, emotionally-charged, event-led approaches), but that the context of relationship enables 'other' to be grappled with like the story of Jacob wrestling the angel (Genesis 32:22-29).

At this point, the groups you have been working with most intently will be comfortable with the risks you have engaged in together, as described in the previous chapter. At this juncture it is about the extension of these challenges and activities so that they have a more deliberate spiritual edge.

In order to enable the young people to engage spiritually you need to first reflect on your own spirituality and theology. You may have wrestled with the character of God, the words of the Bible, the works of God, or theological themes of justice, empowerment, faith, love, hope, and how the young people you work with mirror these themes or attributes. In all these things, be thinking, praying and reflecting on the character of God. Acknowledge His actions and purposes for you and continue to seek these as you journey together with the young people.

When working alongside the young people, you will experience glimpses of spirituality in them. As we are all made in the image of God and are therefore spiritual beings, your encounters with them take on a symbiotic, spiritual, educational journey perspective, rather than a didactic telling, or a simple transfer of 'spiritual' knowledge paradigm. This, in practice, is all part of the risk that symbiotic practice engenders, but how and when is it appropriate to articulate the process of this collaborative spiritual journey? When the kairos moment is not obvious, how do you use the resource of the chronos time invested as a platform to introduce spirituality to the context?

> As part of Football Church, we ran a Friday night football project, and a football team which plays in the FA Christian Football league.

We had approximately one hundred and twenty young people between the ages of eleven and twenty-five come and play football over two different sessions each Friday evening. Through the three years of running the Friday nights, we saw more than three hundred young lads through our doors, journeyed with them and shared our faith through the relationships we built with the lads and their girlfriends/mates.

We would come together to share in the love of football, our lives and pray together before playing football. All of the young people who came knew we were Christians and accepted the prayers offered. The young people were from different backgrounds, of both faith and no faith. The Friday nights worked well like this for two years, but as leaders we kept feeling God's spirit prompting us for more.

We developed a God Spot, utilising some of the material from Ambassadors in Sport, but also developing our own talks. We had some great results, but also some hard times throughout this new venture. We wanted to use this new God Spot as a space to use football as a medium to engage with the Bible and to have conversations with the young people about issues that are relevant to them and football. These sessions worked well, with most of the young people engaging with the talks. However, I noticed that the young people were just giving us 'God answers' when asked a question, so I decided to try another approach.

After lots of time in prayer I decided to run a few sessions without using Church terminology i.e. Church/God/Jesus/worship etc. and see how we would get on without using words that can alienate a group.

I shared a story with them, Imagine....

Imagine you're playing in one of the most important games of the season. You have the ball. You look up and have a clear path up the field. A defender approaches and attempts to tackle you. Using your ball control you have learnt over the years, you easily get round him. Another defender attempts to take you on but you're too quick for him. You look up and have a perfect shot at goal. You fake it left and watch the goalie drop that way before sinking the ball into the top right corner...You score the winning goal and the crowd is going crazy...

What is that feeling inside of you? What would you name it...?

Can you get that feeling any other time? What about if you're having a really bad day?

The lads called this feeling the 'Job Done' feeling. They didn't think it was possible to attain this feeling at any other time, only when you've done something great.

We explored this further, I shared that I get that 'Job Done' feeling all day, even on a bad day. To me that 'Job Done' is the Spirit (though I didn't use so many words).

Over a number of weeks the lads and I shared ideas about what that 'Job Done' feeling was; what it really was.... was it spiritual? If it was, what would it be?

We got the lads to explore it in their own way, in a way that they understood and was relevant to them, then to move on and show them how it could make a difference in their lives.

We actually managed to get the lads excited about what we were talking about, get them to think deeply about it, and to name it...it was now theirs!

The best thing – calling the Holy Spirit the 'Job Done' feeling, and them recognising it in their lives...Awesome!

Ali Simpson-Smith, The Edge Project

Developing a spiritual journey

Aside from carrying out tasks and activities with the small groups, the principal tool you have utilised well to date is that of conversation. Up until this Stage conversation has been used to facilitate, guide and advise. Now is the time to reflect on these things within a more 'spiritual' framework.

As we journey together, we connect with the 'other', the knowable yet unknown God. Kester Brewin, writes the following:

> *To live in harmony, we need only to be constantly putting ourselves in places where we can hear that harmony, hear that divine music that sings of love and says simply this: Dear friends, since God so loved us, we also ought to love. One and other".* [74]

It is in this harmonious relationship, this mutually engaging and symbiotic illustration of us together with the young people encountering 'other', where we can begin to explore spirituality.

Having been through the Risky Small Group Stage, we will know when the time has come to venture further into the realms of spirituality, thereby broadening the relationships we have with the young people. During your time with the young people, you might have had opportunities to discuss faith or spirituality on some level, particularly if you have been upfront with them about your own faith, and therefore to discuss this further will feel like a natural extension of the outworking of your relationship.

One of the most natural ways of doing this within detached work is to use the environment around you or the things you are engaging in. Whatever setting you are in (whether rural or urban, city, town, village, coast or country) there will be resources around you. It could be looking at the stars, the sunsets, rivers (or the absence of them), people, buildings, roads, relationships, journeys – all could be starting points for exploring spirituality with young people. The following questions could be used for opening up conversation:

- People seem to be constantly rushing around here. Do you think being so busy is good for people? Should people stop more to see what's going on around them?

- Some people say that God is everywhere. How might He be here, even in this urban area of man-made structures and concrete?

- When you see the stars, or walk by a river, do you ever wonder why it is all here?

- When you drive your car, how might that be a spiritual experience?

- If God were your friend on Facebook what would he post on your wall every day?

- Is praying something you do and, if so, who do you pray to?

Earlier we talked about the first tool for the journey, the compass of *Culture*, *Tradition* and the *Bible*. This is a useful tool to help us unpack spirituality with the young people. This can be done through the aforementioned use of story. Stories are threaded throughout the lives of individuals, communities and societies. All cultures have story traditions and this is also true of the Christian culture. The stories of 'Flow' and 'Job Done' grew out of the existing culture, tapped into the Christian tradition of storytelling and drew on Biblical narrative. We can tell a story and not need to explain it. We do not dictate how the story is received – to do so would be contrary to Symbiotic Youth Work. We allow the young people to encounter the 'other' within the story and experience it for themselves. How they feel about the story and what they choose to do with it is also up to them.

Another example of how to develop a spiritual journey with young people is the use of ritual: a strong Christian tradition within the church and throughout the Biblical narrative. We in Chard talked to the young people about communion. We took some muffins, blackcurrant squash and some candles down to the skate park. We discussed with them what happens in church with communion, carefully using language to liberate and pace the conversation. By first introducing the young people to the notion of an open spirituality, we can then see they connect this with what 'church' is all about. This is the notion of pacing that we explored earlier – where the worker can change the pace at which things are approached and create an open mutual space. The young people, having taken part in the discussion on communion and using the resources we had brought with us, decided to make a scooter the 'altar' (we had not used that term but they identified it) on which to put the muffins and blackcurrant squash. Later they lit the candles and jumped over then on their bikes, skateboards, or scooters. Allowing space in this way meant that the young people could engage with the process however they chose to, creating their own rituals rooted in their culture.

As discussed earlier, when looking at the role of chronos and kairos (Chapter 17), when those golden 'spiritual' moments appear it is important to act on them. "…even the briefest encounter with a young person can become a moment of meaning as a kairos-moment".[75] The conversation about Flow recorded in Section 1, where we initially suggested Flow might be G-d, was one such moment that happened way before we entered this Stage. Another was when a young person had a toothache and I jokingly suggested we pray, so we did. It could be something as simple as recognising a moment of stillness in a group where people are comfortable with each other and using this to pace the space. As you have already taken risks with the group it is not too big a jump to take a spiritual risk with them.

There may also be obvious times to be 'spiritual': moments of awe and wonder, specific events in the Christian calendar or if a young person has been bereaved (ensuring that you approach such things sensitively). It may be that a young person discloses that they are struggling emotionally. For example, they may be a young carer carrying a lot of practical and emotional responsibility. It is totally appropriate to encourage and support them in this, yet a risky spiritual approach might be to say (in the case of a young carer, for example), "Do you know you're acting like Jesus would in your family? What you're doing is really amazing". This can be a moment not only of encouragement but also space for them to consider what they are doing, the role that they have or the affect they have on others, as something spiritual.

Valuing spiritual questions

You also need to be ready for spontaneous opportunities, even in the everyday and the mundane. Youth worker Jo Dolby gives an example here by explaining how she took an ordinary object and tried to find spiritual meaning through what she termed 'layers of meaning'.

> *During a detached work session a few years ago, some young people were asking me about my experience of God. They seemed eager to experience more of Him, but seemed disappointed that this seemed to always be connected to going to a church building or talking to Christians who they thought were 'a bit weird'. I enjoyed telling them about how God is in everything, that we actually experience God every day without being aware that is what is happening, that everything we do, say, feel, touch, smell and hear is soaked through with God. Everything has layers and layers of hidden meaning, depth and narrative attached to it.*
>
> *On my way to the session I'd stopped to grab a take-away coffee and I still had the cup in my hand. I told them that the cup I held in my hand had hundreds of stories attached to it, hundreds of people all with different lives and interests and hopes and dreams who had all been a part of creating this cup, and that all of that had something of God about it, something we could learn or reflect on. Someone at some point, sat in a room and sketched out the design for what this cup would look like: how big it would be, what it would be made of, where the logo would appear. Someone else was responsible for designing the logo, probably based on research which a few hundred people might have been a part of. Then there was the person who made that coffee for me, who they are, where they're from, what kind of stuff they're facing in their life at the moment. This person made my coffee and gave it to me. So actually, this coffee cup is pretty fascinating. It's not just a coffee cup; it's a storybook. The conversation carried on and eventually all the young people had vanished in different directions trying to find discarded items and lost property around the estate for them to bring back and tell the story of all the people who might have been involved in that particular item being in that particular place on that particular estate. We reflected for a long time on the different meanings and lessons we could draw out from each item, and what those meanings and lessons might say about God.*
>
> **Jo Dolby**

You might find it easier to shape spiritual questions as an idea or through suggestion such as, 'some people think having tattoos is a spiritual expression, what do you think?' or 'so-and-so's music seems to talk about longing and identity, what words would you use if you felt similarly?' of 'if God were part of a car what would He be?'. This disassociation or distancing can help the young people reflect or interact with what you are asking in a more objective, rather than personal way. This is one reason why storytelling is a good medium as it is a creative and non-pressurising approach which young people can engage with on whatever level they want to. They could also be encouraged to associate themselves with the thoughts, characters or feelings in the story. On the streets a more informal approach to storytelling (for example, using tales from your locality) might work well. It may be more appropriate for more formal storytelling to be done in a setting like M&Ms. There are also some resources to help story development. For example you can adapt 'Godly Play', story dice (dice with pictures on them), the Jesus Deck (a Christian card game), or use the FaSt game to explore stories.

Questions or statements shaped in this way may be a good way to find out how open the young people are to spirituality. You might be surprised by their response. Even in relatively Cold Contact moments, Phil Rankin[76] discovered that young people were open to spiritual concepts. So by having a more developed relationship with the young people there should be enough trust in the relationship to respond to your risky spiritual questions. Spiritual actions or rituals could also be used to mark an occasion, celebration, memorial or transitional moment. You could walk around your area and acknowledge the spiritual pictures and images around you – such as bridges, nature, traffic lights, darkness or light, noise or silence, for example. You could also take the young people outside of their context (like the skate pilgrimage), or take those from rural environments to an urban setting and vice versa.

Contemplating spirituality and exploring this with young people will lead you to new places and new understanding with them; this is an inevitable part of the journeying symbiotic relationship. Even as you reframe the Christian story into a new context of which they are part, be that boy-racer gospel, Flow, Job Done or the atonement according to the Goth, they may provide nuanced questions or character that may take you in many spiritual directions. These young people will probably not ask the textbook questions, or even conventional ones, but rather those grounded in their personal attitudes, or often sceptical or technologically shaped minds.

Carpe Diem: 'seize the day'! Enjoy those Kairos moments within your chronos relationship with the young people and expect to be taken to new places and to go off on tangents. As much as the young people trust you, take the risks and follow paths with you, you must also be willing to take those risks and journey with them. This is part of the relationship-building and symbiotic process. It is an exploration that may not have tidy, neat edges and may at times seem chaotic, but it is a process that allows you to learn, seek and find God throughout. It may lead to more questions than answers, but there is no harm in that.

As your relationship is a mutual one, you have to expect that you will need to respond to the same questions you are asking the young people. There is an element of personal risk, in being vulnerable to their questions and thoughts and in exposing your faith to their challenges. Continue to allow space for the young people to explore and play. Interact with their inquisition of God, rather than reducing Him to set, one-dimensional concepts or apologetics.

Exploring spirituality symbiotically with young people is definitely risky and you may feel at times as if you are out of your depth as your own faith is stretched. This is where the symbiotic space expands (or perhaps it will feel as if it is abundant with new possibilities and undreamt of experiences) where we not only expose the young people to new perspectives but where equally we are likewise exposed. Free of Christian jargon, for example we have encountered projects where God has become The Complete, The Boss, Flow or Other, rather than Father or Saviour. They will frame God in their own language. The pictures or narratives you explore with them will be fresh and connected into their own lives and experiences. They will encounter these new spiritual truths in a way that is both familiar and challenging.

Symbiosis in Practice

- Spirituality doesn't just happen at this stage, it will have been embedded throughout your journey;

- Spirituality can be difficult to define;

- Stories can be a good way to engage young people with spirituality;

- Together with the young people, we engage with 'other';

- Use the environment you are in – urban or rural, city, town or village;

- Unpack spirituality within the triangle of Culture, Tradition and the Bible;

- Use story and ritual; and

- Spirituality is not just in the awe and wonder of life, but in the everyday.

3

Chapter 18 – Stage 9: Church on the Edge and Peer Education

> *Gazebo Grapes is a youth-led exploration of spirituality, which grew out of a village, church-based open youth group. The young people are from non-church backgrounds and what they discuss in Gazebo 'church' is youth-led rather than the leaders determining an agenda. It is this fluid quality which allows the workers to respond as they go – dissecting and discussing a whole host of topics and thinking about these from a Christian and non-Christian perspective. It is a journey they and the young people are undertaking together, as the youth worker explained:*

> *"We have been thinking about the Definition of Church and whether the group feel that we are church. What does this group feel like to them? Is what we are doing a new way of being church? Does the fact that we have our gazebo up in a traditional church mean that we are church?"*

> **Tracey Hallett**

> **StreetSpace Chard partnered with St. John's Church Tatworth**

A contemporary vision of church

> *Organizations, the church included, are built to administer, maintain and protect from harm that which already exists; in contrast, creative or dissenting people are designed to give birth to that which has never been in existence before. Thus dissenters threaten the well-oiled structures of an organization's process. The alternatives they propose are seen as chaotic, something to be vigorously avoided by those taking comfort in the predictable and safe ways of tradition.* [77]

Whether it is down to a lack of courage or imagination, as has already been discussed, the contemporary vision of church is often limited. That which seems set in stone, traditional, the way we have chosen to 'be' church, makes it difficult to challenge or question the norm or break out of traditional ways of doing church.

> *... mission helps to burst the old wineskins with the pressure of cross-cultural interpretation, dissolving the barriers of cultural exclusiveness.* [78]

In recent years, the emerging church has helped overcome some of this inertia, but it is important to recognise the domination that the church has over mission, the way we practice our beliefs and the way forward.

When discussing the influence the church had, Vincent Donovan says, "It is not scripture or theology which prevented them from doing what they thought they had a right to do but simply the history of church embedded in a single culture with its own ideas coming from that culture".[79] It would seem here that the church felt it needed a level of protection as the gospel was explored in new cultures. As discussed in the previous chapter, however, we see a more harmonious and imaginative relationship between *Culture*, the *Bible* and *Christian* Tradition.

Up until this Stage, the more conventional detached work and open youth club programme has been discussed. It is at this point we get a greater sense of the new place we inhabit: definitely the place marked on the map as the 'Land of Dragons' – an unexplored landscape of unimagined joys and unexpected thrills. For some of you reading this, you may feel like this is too near the edge, a precarious place that seems too far out of your comfort zone, yet this is what your symbiotic relationships have been unfolding so far and the place we have been travelling towards. Remember, as Rowan Williams asserts, church starts where Jesus is with others. By intentionally setting out to be and grow church with the young people, we have already begun to feel some of the contours of the new place that may well have been genuinely fresh expressions of church/community with the young people for some time. At the same time, the notion of 'peer education', where the young people are peer learners with you and one another, may be a new concept. For symbiotic practice it is important to keep this peer education and use it interchangeably with the Church on the Edge wording, as some young people will reject church as a concept, but remain committed to journeying with you. They may also (as we will see with Gazebo Grapes) completely redefine both church and peer education into something else. If we are genuinely going to be willing to travel to the new place, we need this Stage not to be a fixed end-point but an open expanse to continue onwards.

Nine years ago, Greg was working for a Diocese in the Midlands. He noticed a regular group of Goths hanging out in the city centre near where he worked. They were a group of young people who stood out and attracted unwarranted negative attention – such as being accused of vandalizing a local monument that was defaced with graffiti which depicted nothing to do with the culture of those young people. One day Greg prayed about the young people and the next morning they came to one of the church services. He gave them hot chocolate and chatted to them. They continued to come to the services but unfortunately they weren't always made to feel welcome by other members of the church.

A youth project was set up, linked with the local cathedral and they tried out various things, like Youth Alpha, but the young people weren't really connecting with this in any meaningful way. It was at this juncture that they started to use Compline (a closing of the day reflection): with its simple style, candles and meditative approach, it resonated with their Goth lifestyle.

Since its inception in 2004, this work has now evolved. The youth project has become a separate enterprise, in which some of the original young people are involved. Another venture that has been developed came about when Greg's wife, who at the time had a young child, noticed that a lot of parents with young children were hanging around in the city centre with nowhere to go. They opened up a café in the city centre for parents with young children, some of whom were also part of the original Goth scene in the city. Through the café, they are able to support those in need and at the margins of society.

They planted a church that was a way of linking together the groups from the youth project and the café. They ran a service on Christmas Day 2012 which was a particularly memorable event with generations of families getting together. The day involved feasting together, sharing the Christmas story and saying 'thank you' prayers. This helped move the church forward as it became more purposeful. They are now looking at developing an allotment so that more can get involved, as eating together is an important aspect of what they do and so that those that don't want to prepare the food can help grow it!

This is a long-term project and I'm sure Greg, when he prayed about a group of Goths he saw hanging out on the streets, never imagined it would lead to the work he is involved in today.

'Church' is a contested term, not unlike 'Christian' or even 'youth worker'. What we consider to be 'church' often shapes our mission, our Christology and our theology. Yet this is inherently dangerous given that church can be seen as something of establishment, political and (fallen) human construction, however well-intentioned. As discussed previously, here we are liberating the language of 'church' to open it up to new interpretations, particularly by the young people we are working with.

We began this chapter with the story of Gazebo church/Grapes. The following is a recent discussion between the worker and the young people about church (young people's initials have been changed for confidentiality).

(Tracey) "Do you think we are church?"

(AB) "We cannot be church – we are not religious."

(CE) "Yeah, we are church as we are a body of people together in the community: that makes us church."

(Tracey) "So as we sit under a Gazebo in a traditional church each week, can we call ourselves Gazebo Church?"

(AB) "We are more like a discussion group. Church isn't like that; it is people talking at you. It's not really like you can start asking questions in a church service".

(FH) "We should call ourselves 'The Gazebo Grapes'."

(Tracey) "Why 'Gazebo Grapes'?"

(FH) "Because our discussions could be seen like a 'grapevine' – like 'heard it through the grapevine'! Our group are like grapes attached to the vine (the Gazebo). We are growing together under the Gazebo and we can take it out anywhere into the community."

(PL) "That's a cool metaphor."

(FH) "Yeah, but listen, we could then share our Grapes in the community with others, like at the Summer Fete 'n' stuff; invite people to come into the Gazebo and talk to us. We can give them little bunches of grapes with a nice message attached to them. We could even begin a social enterprise. I am gonna think of a logo".

(Tracey) "That is amazing – let's do it! Perhaps this could be a way forward for a different and new way of being community and church together – taking the Gazebo out and offering 'acts of random kindness'."

(Tracey) "I want to share my thoughts with you. I think that the idea about the vine being the gazebo and the grapes being us growing together is amazing because Jesus says that he is the true vine and God is the gardener. God prunes the branches of the vine when they are not fruitful so that they can begin to grow fruit again. You guys are being very fruitful and when you do share the real grapes with others in the community, it will spread hope and encourage others to also become fruitful too!"

This is one of those kairos moments: when a group of young people exploring together and symbiotically with the leaders come up with not only Biblical imagery but also a Christian value of generosity. It is also worrying that they view traditional church as a place where they cannot ask questions! These types of moments can only be experienced when you take the risk and step out with the young people on a shared journey.

Being in the thick of it

Kevin Vanhoozer begins to help us re-frame church, mission and theology. He outlines the role the universal church has in relation to the Theo-dramatic performance. Theodrama is a way of re-imagining ourselves as participating in the thick of the Gospel action (or drama), not one stage removed from it, by acting and re-performing it in the contexts we are in. This redresses the ever-reducing scientific view of the world by urging us to reaffirm that, "there is no more fertile seedbed for the social imagination than the theodrama of the Christian Gospel. Theology needs more imagination, not less".[80] As 'performers' in the on-going participatory theatre of theodrama, our role is to follow Philip (Acts 8:25-42), guiding those in the searching audience to become performers in new contexts,[81] to participate in new performances with Biblical text (or script) in hand, to improvise creatively and appropriately with this and to translate it for new cultures.[82]

As actors performing in theodrama, we take our place in the fourth act of a five-act play.[i] The fourth act is where the birthing, creating and function of the church takes place and awaits the fifth act: the return of the king.[83] Therefore, to be church is to realise and rehearse the Kingdom of God; loving as Jesus loved, enlarging the stage for new performance to occur, living out the new reality of Jesus. Vanhoozer defines church as, "Interactive theatre where a distinct view of the world – as created for fellowship with the triune God – is remembered, studied, cultivated and celebrated in corporate performance".[84]

If we are, as Vanhoozer suggests, to imagine church as our involvement in a performance, that we become part of the action, we could further this to incorporate our role not only of actor, but also of spect-actor. Augusto Boal, a pioneering theatre practitioner working with the marginalised and oppressed in Brazil, developed the concept of the spect-actor, which he describes in his book *Theatre of the Oppressed*.[85] By removing the barrier between actor and audience, Boal has created a theatre – or we could say here, 'church' – that enables the spectator to influence what is performed on stage or how church is encountered. Spectators become 'spect-actors', able to directly engage and participate in the production and exploration of theatre. So we can not only actively engage with this new envisioning of church, but also step outside of it and become

---

[i] This 'act' analogy was originally developed by N.T. Wright, which is explored in several of his publications.

objective observers. To build on this we would argue that, by the young people becoming involved in this symbiotic journey of church, not only do they change what church looks like but also they themselves are changed through the process.

So what might all this theatre and theodrama mean in the youth work context? In reality what you have being doing so far is 'enlarging' the stage by being physically, symbiotically with young people on the streets, or creating a space in a building. With them, you have enlarged and liberated the scope of the stage from the confines of church buildings, to include this travelling community of young people and leaders. Vanhoozer determines that, "the world is our stage",[86] yet this can only be if we as Christians are in it. As the symbiotic relationship has developed with the young people, they have become encouraged to be participants in the imaginative theodrama through the process of accepting you and the exploration of community, spirituality and life.

We previously looked at how church is a "community of friends"[87] and how church is a place where stories, tragedies and celebrations are shared. You together with the young people, in symbiosis, as a community of friends, explore Christian spirituality in the day-to-day life of the community as it celebrates, remembers and hurts, as young people articulate stories of faith. All of this is church: church on the edge of organised church, church on the edge of community; but no less 'church'! It is a church that has a purpose of continuing the holistic redemptive processes that it has started in relationships with young people and rooted in the relational G-d of the Trinity. It is a church that is being and becoming, no longer a physical structure but at heart a movement of reconciled people: reconciled to one another and reconciled to Jesus. It is a social, ethnic and racial reconciliatory church which corresponds to the contours of the new creation.[88] As young are reconciled to old; as their own relationships are reconciled; as regard grows for others, for the environment and for the world then active reconciliation occurs that is both worshipful and Kingdom-presenting.

As a youth worker you have followed the apostolic role of Philip (Acts 8:26-40) whom, on the Gaza road helped the Ethiopian eunuch to see the old text in a new way, by sharing with him the person of Jesus. "There is always something forgotten that can be remembered and something not yet learned that can be discovered".[89] Your role has been to draw alongside, to work symbiotically with the young people, to open up the space for thoughts and questions, to encourage social, emotional and spiritual reflection and consider possible interpretations of traditional narratives. You have interpreted the Word with the young people as together you interacted with it, at times explaining the culture and context within which it takes place (as explained earlier with the story of the wedding feast), always offering them a way to appropriately engage with and translate the Word.

Philip accepts the Ethiopian and responds to his desire for belonging by baptising him. Like the Ethiopian, some of the young people you work with may have been mistreated or ignored by the established church. It is in this moment of movement from isolation to acceptance that the Ethiopian is baptised and goes on his way rejoicing – going to the familiar, yet now new context of his homeland.

So at what point does Stage 8 become Stage 9: Church on the Edge? Changes or developments will be subtle and the evolution of the group, although perhaps instigated by you, will have been collectively agreed. In Exploring Spirituality with the young people you may have developed a spiritual understanding of a context or activity, such as skateboarding, football, car-driving or other outdoor activities. As these conversations continue, it may seem appropriate to articulate the notion of naming the group within church language such as Curry Church, Car Park Church or Play Church. If the group do not find it appropriate to use the word church and are more comfortable with terms like 'group' or 'community', then it is important to respect that. Using the language of church will allow you to explore with them what church might mean (as seen in Gazebo Grapes earlier) and how the church you have co-created symbiotically is an on-going movement of people exploring faith, reconciling relationships and belonging; a pilgrim church with ceremonies that mark belonging, tragedy and celebration.

A further indication that the created church community is becoming and evolving church is when the young people propose actions or ceremonies of faith with you in their context – hence the inter-changeability with peer education. Like the Ethiopian was empowered and released through a newly discovered interpretation that drew him to Jesus, he went to his own land and context to do the same with others. Within the safe space you have created symbiotically, the young people may also want to articulate their faith. This could be by sharing a prayer or poem, illustrating their faith through a story or picture, their outward actions towards friends (or enemies), the sharing of gifts or food, concern for global or local injustice: all could be interpreted as acts of worship, recognising the signs of the Kingdom here and now. Where spiritual exploration started with a question, and may have become an exploration at your instigation, it has gone full circle to become something the young people actively pursue with you symbiotically as a collaborative learning experience with their community of friends.

The young people may go on from this exploration to form groups or clusters which effectively continue this spiritual learning experience, drawing ever closer to encounters with Jesus, being together and journeying together as pilgrim church. These groups may include certain activities akin to worship, prayer and reflection. These can be developed with the young people after spending some time exploring what this means to them, as part of the on-going process. Opportunities may now exist to develop these ideas into creative responses and actions that are appropriate to the context, further providing young people with the opportunity to express themselves.

So Church on the Edge remains an evolving place as well as place of homecoming. It is a place where the young people feel comfortable to explore spirituality with their friends. It is a place of community and learning, a place of remembering, of reconciling and celebrating, a place where they encounter G-d in their midst. However, it is not a static or a fixed place where you and the young people go to encounter 'other'. Seeing Church on the Edge as a fixed place would lead to the same dualistic traps we mentioned earlier – the separation of being and doing. It is a place where missional spirituality is shared by the young people and becomes part of their way of looking at the world. This is a place not much different to the post-resurrection stories told by the disciples. As they walked to Emmaus (Luke 24:35-53) or fished on the lake (John 21:1-26), Jesus revealed himself to them in familiar places (the beach and their homes) and in those places they remembered, celebrated, shared, were reconciled and were commissioned to further work. Maybe the narratives of these early disciples – meeting Jesus and figuring out what to do amid the dominant culture of the religious order of the day – provides inspiration and example for you as the emerging church symbiotically continues to be church at the edge of a culture and an institutional church.

Symbiosis in Practice

- We are in the Land of Dragons!
- Getting to this point has been about yours and the young people's commitment to the journey;
- Redeem/liberate the word 'church';

- Do theodrama – get involved in the action, immerse yourself in the big story of G-d's redeeming mission;

- We are a 'community of friends' – a place to share stories, tragedies and celebrations;

- When young people propose actions or ceremonies of faith with you in their context – this is church; and

- Church on the Edge is always evolving.

3

Section 4:
Base Camp

4

Chapter 19 – Preparing for Symbiotic Practice

You can only stretch a metaphor so far and in an ideal world we could get on with being symbiotic, but we recognise that often the people we are accountable to want facts and figures. Our supporters, funders, partners and stakeholders like to be able to measure the impact we are having and may even set some of the criteria. It is a challenge to balance the demands of measuring the impact whilst still holding true to our values and missional approach. This section is where we step aside from the Land of Dragons to consider the mixed youth work context we find ourselves in. We need to think pragmatically about finding a balance, which enables us to keep the work going without compromising the distinctive ethos of a symbiotic approach. Therefore, this section looks at some of the broader issues relating to good practice. It has already been noted how youth work values and Symbiotic Youth Work go hand in hand, so with this in mind we need to consider areas from practice that can support the work we do and in turn, how working within these frames of reference helps local projects communicate the work being done to the wider youth work community. This will give a level of confidence to outside agencies and funders that the work is well thought through, managed and monitored.

Getting started

The concept of Symbiotic Youth Work recognises the shifting theological and cultural landscape that demands fresh approaches. However, in broader terms, how do you determine the need for a youth work project in the first place? There may be a sense of calling that is incumbent on all of us to serve the local community and others, to work towards shalom and wholeness and that for you this is best done through developing youth work.

Symbiotic Youth Work is not a programme you can buy off the shelf, but more of a story and values system put into practice. The stories shared have come from different projects, approaches and contexts. How do you determine what sort of project structure is right for what you need to develop locally? At a practical, organisational level, how do you begin to discover what the missio Dei is already doing? What questions need asking? Who do you ask? What structures are needed? How will you manage, communicate and fund the work? The national StreetSpace Community of Practice through FYT can provide further resources which can help you work through these questions, but whatever you decide there will be many practicalities that need to be considered.

4

Community audits and mission statements

A helpful place to start as you develop your project is with a community audit or profile where local services, organisations, needs and opportunities are assessed in a thorough and organised way. A Symbiotic Youth Work approach demands that any community profiling process involves young people as much as possible. Assuming you have already identified a basic need for the project and begun to develop some values based around your hopes and dreams, you will need to consider what fits where and the type of structure and organisation needed. In reality, StreetSpace is a community of dispersed groups who coalesce around shared values, the practical out workings of which have evolved into the concept of Symbiotic Youth Work.

Mission statements

Most groups will have a mission statement outlining what it is that they want to do. A local project rooted in a symbiotic approach might say, "XYZ project seeks to work with young people towards their personal, social and spiritual development, through a range of opportunities and activities that are mutually developed with young people and underpinned by the values of empowerment, participation, equality and education".

This mission statement may be further refined over time as you research local community needs, geography, issues and gather around you others who share your vision. But do not be tempted to just copy another group's mission statement: your mission statement needs to hold true to your local context and values.

Organisational structure

The next step is to consider the type of organisational structure that can best facilitate what you are seeking to do and who can help make that a reality. There could well be an organisation already in place or you may be part of a wider body of people, for example an established church, which can host what you are doing.

If you need to set up something new, there are essentially three sorts of organisational structures (charities, community associations, and community interest companies) that may facilitate what you are trying to achieve. You will need people with the appropriate skills depending on which structure you choose.

All of these structures will require some sort of governing document that sets out:

- What you are trying to do;
- Who you are aiming at;

4

- The powers and restrictions of the group; and
- Procedures for meetings, members, finances, changing the document and closing down.

The organisational structure will put into place a level of oversight and the beginnings of a management process in terms of financial accounts, decision-making and planning. However, you also need a level of line management and support. The pressure and difficulties workers will face should not be underestimated. Earlier we spoke about Arbuckle's view of dissent: essentially you are looking for someone with the heart of an authority dissenter but with the skills to cope with a pathfinder who will be firing off ideas and running ahead. It is important to bear in mind that you are working within the compass of *Bible*, *Culture* and *Tradition* and reimagining church within this. It can be difficult for managers to put to one side their bias towards one compass point, particularly if they have a strong *Bible* or *Tradition* focus.

4

Chapter 20 – The Three Ps: Project Management, Policies and Procedures

I couldn't believe it when I first saw the house. I had heard shouting and screaming in the next street whilst on my way home. As I turned the corner I saw Jim, who I knew well and would tell me what had happened. The house was wrecked: the windows smashed, the door kicked in, fence torn down, drainpipes ripped off. It looked like there had been a hurricane. I knew the family who lived there and the oldest boy, Scott, who no one tangled with.

Scott was as hard as they come and was scary as he punched first and rarely thought about the consequences. His mum had had a difficult time bringing up three boys on her own and they were pretty challenging. Scott, who was the oldest at sixteen, had been expelled from school for fighting and never tried to go to another; the younger two were eight and four(ish). Jim told me that the youngest boy had been accused of trying to rape a neighbouring girl his age. What had happened was unclear but the girl's extended family had jumped into action the previous day and had run the family off the estate. Scott was now riding around the estate with a baseball bat, ready to batter any of the extended family he could find. The commotion earlier was because he had just gone past taunting those in the street that knew him.

Richard Passmore

It is beyond the scale of this publication to go into all the detail required to fully cover all policy and management issues. What is offered here are some broad observations about core issues. Even this cannot be seen as an exhaustive list but simply a start point[i]. The reality is that you may encounter challenging circumstances in the Land of Dragons and, whilst you cannot legislate for everything, policies and procedures accompanied by good project management are essential to help you move forward.

Dealing with risk

The situation described above was eventually concluded, but dealing with real people is risky. As youth workers we are putting ourselves at risk: risking our actions being misinterpreted, risking violence, risking rejection and accusation. In *Meet them where they're at*, Pip Wilson's poem was used to highlight some of the reasons why risk is

4

---

[i] There are many groups that can offer support in these areas, such as local voluntary community councils, AMAZE, diocesan youth officers (or equivalent) and FYT.

important and also why risk is important in the symbiotic process.

To laugh is to risk appearing the fool
To weep is to risk appearing sentimental
To reach out is to risk involvement
To expose feelings is to risk exposing your true self
To place your ideas and dreams before the crowd is to risk their love
To love is to risk not being loved in return
To live is to risk dying
To hope is to risk despair
To try is to risk failure
But the greatest hazard in life is to risk nothing
The one who risks nothing does nothing and has nothing and finally is nothing
He may avoid suffering and sorrow,
But h/she simply cannot learn, feel, change, grow or love
Chained by certitude, he is a slave, he has fortified freedom.
Only the one who risks is free!
Author unknown

Without risk there can be no pathfinding dissenters but, as responsible adults often working with vulnerable young people, we need to expect the unexpected and be as prepared as possible for what lies ahead by developing appropriate policies and procedures. The StreetSpace community of practice regularly reviews policies, adapting and developing them to fit symbiotic practice. For example, often the idea of lone working is actively discouraged by organisations. In a bid to remain safe and at a professional distance, the humanity of the encounters needed to meet real people with real need is in danger of being completely removed.

It is important to prepare appropriate risk assessments for the areas you are working in. A helpful start point is to develop one for regular sessions. This should cover all the areas you are working in as well as identifying any risks associated with travel to, from and between locations. Thinking about some of the issues in advance can give the space that symbiotic practice needs whilst also keeping young people and staff safe.

Reducing harm

'Harm reduction' is a method used to reduce the risks to young people engaged in various activities. It is primarily informal education based in a youth work context and helps people be aware of the dangers associated with particular activities.

The example below is an approach used which aims to reduce the harm from drug use.

Harm reduction is an approach to education. It works by:

- Providing accurate and correct information about drug use and its risks.
- Developing the skills for safer drug use.
- Promoting more accepting attitudes towards drug users.
- Encouraging existing and would-be drug users to discover safer ways of using and thus reducing the harm of drug use.
- Encouraging people to use less harmful drugs, or combinations of drugs, and possible abstinence.

Matt had been a prime contact. I had known him for several years and it was strange that he was now working. We had done a lot together: planned a trip to Drayton Manor theme park, raised money for a camp and talked about a lot of family issues. We had often talked about his family events, as they seemed quite a laugh. Matt had a large extended family and always had some funny story to relate. I wish I could tell stories like he could. Someone would have fallen off the table whilst dancing or collapsed in a heap. His dad even fell asleep in the wardrobe one night.

Alcohol was always part of the stories and usually the reason why something had happened. Now Matt was older and off doing his own thing, I would hear stories of what he had been up to on the previous weekend. At sixteen he was working and he was drinking both with his mates from work and friends who I knew through detached work.

Although he could tell a great story and joke, he wasn't overly popular. He would always end up doing something memorable when he got drunk. He had fallen through a window, ripped a tent in two, done the full Monty and now, as we chatted, his hand was bandaged as he had got into a fight at a nightclub. It would take a long time to bring Matt to a realisation that, whilst he wasn't an alcoholic, getting drunk wasn't doing him any good. We explored areas of self-esteem, some of the old family stories, and he agreed to try not to get so drunk and to accept responsibility for his actions. In the end I moved on and needed to get a co-worker to continue supporting him.

Richard Passmore

4

In *Meet them where they're at*, we discussed harm reduction, which was a new concept to many workers at the time. The questions we must ask relating to harm reduction, as with many of the other issues encountered when working with young people on the edge, centre around our role as a worker. Should we accept, transform or live with the tension between these two approaches? Are we:

1. Condoning their behaviour?
2. Conforming to their culture?
3. Challenging their situation?

Hopefully we have explained enough of Symbiotic Youth Work to know that it moves us beyond these easy distinctions. Symbiosis is about dialogue and mutuality that develops as you explore with young people the issues around their behaviour and how this can help re-found community and church.

In the issues we have raised so far we have identified that projects will need to consider risk, child protection and staff safety. Depending on your local areas and project you may require specific policies relating to, for example, prostitution, theft and violence.

Confidentiality

Confidentiality is an important issue for all youth work contexts. The mutuality of the relationships that you are trying to establish adds another dimension to this. As youth workers needing to keep young people safe, it is never possible to promise total confidentiality as if the information disclosed puts the young people or others at risk you may need to action your safeguarding process. In order to facilitate building community and symbiotic approaches it may be helpful to have an open confidentiality policy where issues are shared within the team and/or with other professional agencies when needed.

A symbiotic approach should be as young person-centred as possible. Confidentiality can be maintained within the team rather than resting with the individual worker unless there is a legal duty to inform a third party or a worker is subpoenaed. This releases individuals from the weight of an issue that can be better carried by the team as a whole.

It is important to realise we are not alone. There are many specialist agencies that can offer information and support. Your community profile may have highlighted such agencies in your area. When referring young people to another agency, it is important to include them in the process and discuss each step with them – this is where the symbiotic approaches need to be grounded in the reality of the context. Passing a young person on to another agency does not relieve you of your responsibility to that young person. It may be helpful to go with them as they develop a supportive network for themselves as part of their unfolding of a new community.

4

The pain and hurt that is faced by young people going through difficulties should not be underestimated. It also offers space for growth and change. Therefore, it is helpful to build a network of contacts that you know and trust and are happy to refer young people onto. This may include a drug agency, a counselling service, a homelessness project, a lawyer, a doctor who is not in the area and a sexual health clinic. Where possible, visit these places and try to get to know someone there who may be sympathetic to the aims of your project. Check out their confidentiality procedures and explain your aims, finding out what provision can be made out of normal hours.

Although we have raised several policy areas for you to consider, ultimately all of the above is about having the right project management processes. It is pointless to have policies without appropriate procedures for workers to follow. These policies and procedures need to be updated and reviewed regularly and it must be clear who within the management team will take responsibility for this. As we try to practically bed-in Symbiotic Youth Work, it is important that the values of mutuality and empowerment are mirrored at all levels of the organisation, including management level.

Space for symbiosis at all levels

Asking questions about how young people can participate in developing policies and procedures is vital. The young people may not be able to contribute through formal committee meetings. Therefore projects must explore creative ways to bring young people into management decisions by looking at how meetings can be reshaped to enable young people to attend, or how workers can facilitate young people's views to be heard. In some ways this comes back to what was said in the opening chapters about the local project in Chard starting with a team of two going out on the street. This helped the project to be open at the edges, to help the young people feel part of the community, where the leaders could develop and see the project grow symbiotically. However, the challenge for Chard is that it is still managed by adults over eighteen for legal reasons. Viewed from the outside, the committee could be seen as the core of the project, when in fact the management committee, workers and young people need to explore ways together as to how they can foster more genuine community.

4

Chapter 21 – Monitoring and Evaluation

One particular aspect of project management that is likely to be your responsibility is how you keep records, what you measure and how. In Symbiotic Youth Work, how do you measure change, development and growth? Who does the measuring and what relationship does this have with funders, managers, and those cheering you on from the side-lines?

Essentially, there are three broad areas that need to be covered:

- Recording what is happening in each session.
- Monitoring progress and the processes used.
- Evaluating the outcomes of the work that impact young people and the wider community context.

Thinking about and demonstrating change

Ultimately Symbiotic Youth Work is about managing change, so it is important that your organisation identify its theory of change. For example, youth workers generally believe that open provision has an impact on young people by helping them to become better citizens, to grow as individuals and to build confidence. This is historically the anecdotal basis that much work has been based on with countless stories of how youth work has had a positive effect on young people.

> Fred, a young person we had known since the start of the project over six years ago, had always wanted to become a tree surgeon. His dream was to go to Canada as a logger. Fred had a difficult time at school and it was obvious from the stories he told that his lively attitude was likely to clash with secondary school authorities. He spent much of his time out of school and when we met him at seventeen years old he had left school and had a few temporary farming jobs, but nothing had stuck.

> At eighteen he had tried a few factory jobs that, quite frankly, he hated and to which he was unsuited. He had struggled with sitting still in classrooms and found factories were little different. Whenever we saw him he used to say he wanted to work outside. At nineteen he started getting more serious about retraining and became a young leader with us. At twenty he moaned about not being able to get to do tree surgery as he could not get an apprenticeship. At twenty one he finally got on a course. Last week at the skate park, I have never seen a happier Fred – holding down a job, passing his course and even staying on to do an extra year to raise his skills set.
> **Richard Passmore**

4

Throughout the process we actively encouraged and challenged Fred. We supported the development of his social and leadership skills through his involvement in young leaders. We encouraged him, offered him lifts to college interviews, discussed the future and encouraged some more. We played our part in the process, but the question is how do you show this or even; do we need to? For many projects, negotiating the reality of finding continued funding means a need to demonstrate the outcomes they have achieved with young people. This creates a tension within symbiotic practice as starting with outcomes or targets means you can miss the heartbeat of symbiosis, and we need to think about how we negotiate this.

If as Ord suggested outcomes are not accidental, what evidence do you need to gather? How can you record this to show that there is a link between the open youth club, detached work, shed loads of encouragement and the positive outcome for Fred or the countless others mentioned? The Young Foundation[i] discusses this, as the lead agency of Catalyst, a consortium tasked to explore the impact of youth work. They identified and developed seven clusters of capabilities that are of value to all young people in terms of their social and emotional capacities and suggest that the development of these social and emotional capabilities are often at the heart of good youth work.

The Young Foundation clearly identify that these social and emotional outcomes not only affect the individual but also the social context of the young people, having an intrinsic and extrinsic impact. They developed a matrix in four boxes identifying the relatedness and impact that the social and emotional capabilities had on broader outcomes such as: benefits to society, interpersonal relationships and individual achievements and behaviours. These attributes also relate well to the Scottish curriculum for evidence which focuses on well-being, problem solving, contribution to community and achievement. Wales and Northern Ireland also have their own dedicated youth work curriculum. The various youth work agendas from the different nations all seek to outline the benefits that youth work has to wider society. In Fred's case, the encouragement, support and opportunity he had through becoming a young leader impacted and developed his social and emotional capability. This in turn impacted his individual achievement making him a benefit to society.

4

---

[i] The Young Foundation was responding to a particular government agenda at a particular time. However, the work is well researched and evidenced, with a strong theoretical backdrop and evidence base. It may be useful beyond a change of government policy.

Symbiotic Youth Work and the Young Foundation's work

The evidence base of the Young Foundation's work on the clusters strongly suggests that mutuality with young people is key, that good youth work unfolds a better society and community for all – it's symbiotic!! The issue is; how can you show the impact your work is having without getting pulled towards outcomes driven practice – i.e. developing work to achieve specific targets without losing the relational heart of symbiosis?

The seven social and emotional capabilities that are put forward by The Young Foundation[i] are:

- Managing Feelings: reviewing, being more self-aware, reflecting, self-regulating, self-accepting
- Communication: explaining and expressing yourself, presenting, listening, questioning, finding alternative ways of communicating
- Confidence and Agency: this is about self-reliance and self-esteem enabling you to be able to shape your own life and the world around you
- Planning and Problem-solving: being able to navigate the resources around you, organise yourself, make decisions, critically analyse and think about risk
- Relationships and Leadership: thinking about the contributions of the whole team and how one another interact, making sure that you can manage any conflict that may arise creatively
- Creativity: the ability to imagine alternative ways of doing things and apply this to a variety of contexts (creativity helps people become more enterprising, innovative, and remain open to new possibilities)
- Resilience and Determination: being self-disciplined, self-controlled and self-motivating, being able to self-manage and concentrate, having a good sense of purpose, being persistent when necessary

It is easy to see how good symbiotic approaches support these seven outcomes clusters, mutually unfolding better individuals and societies, and their intrinsic and extrinsic value. Young people's individual achievements and behaviours will be strengthened and developed as you support their social and emotional capabilities.

4

---

[i] *'Noticing The Change – A Framework of Outcomes for Young People in Practice'*, by Mhairi Aylott, Bethia McNeil Tessa Hibbert, March 2013, published by The Young Foundation.

Young people will be better equipped to develop numeracy, literacy and language skills and have the confidence to gain qualifications. They will be better able to participate and attend work or school and other youth activities. They will take on board advice and develop good support systems around them, having a platform that will enable them to be critical about their choices and behaviour. There should be less need for health services as young people consider more healthy lifestyles and contribute more to the labour market as their social and emotional capabilities develop, helping them to hold down jobs. As they are able to cope with what life throws at them, they will become less dependent on the welfare system and less likely to come into contact with the criminal justice system. The overall benefits to society will be greatly improved and the community will be further strengthened as the young people take more of a lead in their communities. Young people will also become more confident in their social and emotional capabilities, resulting in stronger interpersonal relationships which will in turn help them, if they have children of their own, to become more positive parents. More positive family relationships will help to create a general atmosphere and climate for stronger community cohesion.

One thing we have found really interesting in our local work is the number of young people willing to help at events. We have worked with seven young people who have gone through our young leaders programme, but there are also a further twenty who will help us when we need them. This is the impact of Symbiotic Youth Work that goes beyond the social and emotional capabilities that the Catalyst consortium has researched.

There are two key differences that help us maintain a symbiotic approach. Firstly, that Symbiotic Youth Work recognises that, as we journey with young people, these changes happen to us as well as to them. Secondly, that we value process as much as outcome, so the clusters provide a frame of reference that can be used retrospectively. We will engage with young people following the missio Dei, then reflecting on the groups and individuals see where they fit within the clusters. As we do not take a baseline measurement of where a young person is when we first meet them, it is not until they are further involved in the process that we can see how they have progressed: as indicated earlier, we see outcomes as incidental rather than accidental.

In their most recent publication, *Noticing the change – A framework of outcomes for young people in practice*[90] published in March 2013, The Young Foundation highlighted ten top tips to consider when beginning to measure and evaluate your work. These include;

4

- Considering which outcomes to measure before deciding how to measure them;

- Ensuring that outcomes are understood and realistic within your timeframe; and

- Considering how you and the young people are best involved in the process of defining and measuring the outcomes and using a range of staff from across the organisation.

The publication makes clear that there are a lot of tools to help you measure the outcomes for projects, but that at present the seven clusters of capabilities are still very new. It is expected that these clusters will become the mainstay of outcomes for youth work in the future and they have already been written into local authority guidance. However, whilst this means it is still early days and there are a range of measurement tools available online, it can be difficult to select the right one and also these may change with governments.

StreetSpace is just about ahead of the game, as we have developed a new measurement tool that is more reflective of our symbiotic approach. We recognised the need to integrate the clusters and develop good practice and measurement tools that were appropriate to symbiotic practice. As such we adopted the seven outcomes of social and emotional capabilities alongside our nine stages earlier than most, and have built a strong track record of using these creatively. We are also the only agency (that we know of) that uses them in a group work context rather than just measuring individual progress, which is important in a symbiotic context.

Measurement tools

StreetSpace set the seven social and emotional capabilities in a wheel, which is correlated to the nine-stage process discussed. This is an important part of what differentiates our symbiotic approach from others: we have ensured that the way we measure outcomes is connected to process, as this brings the values-driven approach back to the fore and holds it all in balance. It enables young people and the workers to be mutually embedded in the process. The symbiotic connection of process and outcome then enables local projects to plan and measure what they are doing. In Fred's case, we could have scored him individually against each capability and measured his progress as we did a lot of one to one work with him. However, we measured the progress of him and his peers as a group. At sixteen he was at stage 1-3 when we had just contacted him and his friends. At eighteen, stage 6 as he and his friends came on trips. By the time he and his group did the young leaders training they were into stage 9. So what we were able to do was score the whole group against the capabilities. For example, one thing we recognised with this small group of young men (who we had worked with for a long time and who had been through the leadership programme), was that they scored very highly for all the capabilities except Managing Feelings, so this gave us a sense of some of the work we needed to develop with them. Some may argue that in doing so we are working to an outcomes agenda and have lost any notions of symbiosis. However we would argue that it is all part of the compass and helps us discern what we feel the missio Dei is doing in the lives of individuals and groups. What this process and outcome system does is work in a way that enables us to communicate progress to young people and outside agencies, whilst at the same time evoke a sense of process that is open to G-d, and one another, as the new community/church unfolds.

Records and evidence

Recognising for ourselves the interrelatedness between the process of good, mutual, generic work with young people and outcomes is a good start point, but we also need to communicate this to possible funders, managers and others. It is important to recognise that any tool can become a blunt instrument and we need to consider if the tools that we develop provide us with enough information to fully measure what it is that we are trying to achieve. In terms of StreetSpace, you could argue that the recording sheets we use at the end of every session are gathering the evidence of what is happening and this provides a good indication of the outputs of the organisation, for example, numbers of young people contacted, numbers of sessions and any other observations. The use of the nine stages that are assessed each term – by both local project workers and a StreetSpace worker – help monitor the progress of groups. The data gathered at these termly meetings, and some of the details in the recording sheets, provide the mechanisms to evaluate the impact of the work against the seven capabilities and the broader outcomes. These include benefits to society, individual achievements and interpersonal skills. They will become apparent as you go through the unfolding story recorded in the session recording sheets and identify, for example, when young people found work, moved into training or kept out of trouble with the police.

Therefore, keeping a record of youth work sessions is essential. It enables you to keep track, reminds you of names and events, and protects you when questions are asked. There are two basic types of recording used in our work. The first is a general diary that is kept for every session. This is a record of general information relating to

4

the session. It should contain information on the location worked in, date and time of session, workers present, weather, contacts made with young people and contacts made with other members of the community. A general description of the evening, with issues raised and future action to be taken, should also be included. Reflection is an important technique in youth work. It helps workers recognise recurring issues, personal weaknesses, track the history of contacts and maintain a clear perspective of the current situation. So much information is shared and so many things happen over a long period of time that recording becomes an essential tool in youth work.

The second type of recording is an incident form. These forms should contain more detail and are used when a dangerous or illegal situation has occurred during a session. The aim of the incident form is to record in detail the incident, the action taken by the young people, the response of the worker and the motivation behind the response. The form helps to protect the worker if their action is later questioned.

We encounter surprising situations in youth work and there may be people in the area that are not supportive of your project. It is essential to act responsibly and professionally and take steps to protect yourselves as well as the young people.

In symbiotic practice we recognise that on one level we go into the work with an agenda and some outcomes in mind. However, this agenda is about unfolding a new way of being and growing church/community and we do not know what this will look like and are not manipulating young people towards this. Likewise the outcomes are about enhanced capabilities, recognising that reciprocal relationships play a key role in enabling the outcomes to be achieved, and that these social and emotional capabilities are rooted in kingdom values that drive Symbiotic Youth Work which help us and the young people move towards fullness of life.

4

Chapter 22 – The Continuing Journey

Symbiotic Youth Work and mission is a paradigm-changer in that you have to leave behind your old ideas around church and mission and embrace the new paradigm as you enter the Land of Dragons. We have tried to outline the symbiotic concept but stressed the need to feel your way into this new land. What we have uncovered is the need to be intentional about the process but not prescriptive about the outcome, the need to embed spirituality throughout the whole process and in who you are as a person.

In Section One we highlighted the need for fresh approaches and we unpacked some of the issues and implications of these in Section Two, exploring particular implications for youth work. As we moved into Section Three we began to see what Symbiotic Youth Work looks like in practice and in Section Four we looked at some of the issues behind the scenes, including balancing a symbiotic approach with an outcomes-driven youth work landscape.

This book has presented the idea that we need to unfold a new story mutually with the young people and communities we serve and it has shared stories of people living this way connected through the StreetSpace community of practice. As we tried to conclude this book we realised this was potentially an impossible task, as the journey is still unfolding and we need others to help it continue to develop.

We hope that these stories have challenged the way you look at the world, community, church and faith. We believe Symbiotic Youth Work and mission asks questions that you can only answer on the road, embracing a 'road spirituality' rather than a 'petrol station spirituality', that it is open, joined up, missional, professional, connected, real, messy, joyous, challenging and unfolding. Symbiotic Youth Work take us beyond – it is beyond the modernist lenses towards a both/and spirituality, beyond church and mission to a non-dualistic being/doing, beyond old debates of youth work or youth ministry towards a journey with young people into a third space. It unfolds a space that is changing as we go, changed as we enter and a space that gifts to us the resources to change ourselves. Symbiotic Youth Work is not billed as a deficit model that sees us as the bringers of truth to a community that needs something. Symbiotic Youth Work enters a community space in the full knowledge that this is a sacred, shared space, full of potential, full of G-d, and that only by being in that space can we truly discover wholeness.

4

References

Endnotes

[1]Passmore, R. (2003). *Meet them where they're at: Helping churches engage young people through detached youth work.* Bletchley: Scripture Union.

[2] McClaren, B. (2013). *The Story We Find Ourselves In: Further Adventures of a New Kind of Christian: Book 2.* San Francisco: Jossey-Bass.

[3] Pimlott, J. and Pimlott, N. (2008). *Youth Work After Christendom.* Bletchley, Milton Keynes.

[4] Ibid, p.4-5.

[5] Bevans, S. B. and Schroeder, R. (2004). *Constants in Context: A Theology of Mission for Today.* Maryknoll: Orbis Books. p.34

[6] Sacks, J. (2006). *To Heal a Fractured World: The Ethics of Responsibility.* London:Continuum International publishing group Ltd.

[7] Arbuckle, G. A. (1993). *Refounding the Church: Dissent for Leadership.* Maryknoll: Orbis Books.

[8] Ibid, p.6-7.

[9] Ibid, p.101.

[10] Rollins, P. (2011). *Insurrection: To Believe Is Human to Doubt, Divine.* New York: Howard Books. pp.141-143.

[11] Donovan, V.J. (1996). *Christianity Rediscovered.* London: SCM Press.

[12] Minear, P. S. (2004). *Images of the Church in the New Testament.* Lousiville: Westminster John Know Press.

[13] Eckhart, M. (n.d.). *It is not necessary to understand this.* Available at: www.jeanbouchartdorval.com/jardin/meckhart52-imp.html

[14] Biology-online. *Symbiosis.* Available at: www.biology-online.org/dictionary/Symbiosis

[15] Stiver, D, R. (1994). *The Uneasy alliance between evangelicalism and postmodernism: a reply to Thiselton.* Paper presented at the Southeastern Regional, March 25-26, 1994, Louisville, Kentucky.

[16] Moltman, J. (1977). *Church in the Power of the Spirit.* London: SCM Press. p.64.

[17] Bosch, D.J. (1991). *Transforming Mission: Paradigm Shifts in Theology of Mission.* Maryknoll: Orbis Books. p.472

[18] Ibid.

[19] Lings, G. (2012). *Why Modality and Sodality thinking is vital to understand future church.* Available at: www.churcharmy.org.uk/ms/sc/sfc_talks.aspx

[20] Graham, E. Walton, H. and Ward, F. (2005) *Theological Reflection: Methods.* London: SCM Press.

[21] Richardson, A. (1935). *Creeds in the Making: Short Introduction to the History of Christian Doctrine.* London: SCM Press. p.14

[22] Muers with Ford. (2005). *The Modern Theologians: An Introduction to Christian Theology since 1918.* Chicester:Wiley-Blackwell pp.572-586.

[23] Rollins, P. (2006). *How (not) to speak of God.* London: SPCK. pp.23-25.

[24] Brewin, K. (2011). *Other: Embracing Difference in a Fractured World.* London: Hodder and Stoughton.

[25] Ibid, p.108.

[26] Blower, S. (2012) *Towards a B-boy Theology.* Diss. Bristol: Centre for Youth Ministry.

[27] Ibid, p.9

[28] Ibid, p.48

[29] Ibid, Brewin, K. (2011). p.124.

[30] Bey,H. (1991). *The Temporary Autonomous Zone, Ontological Anarchy, Poetic Terrorism.* Available at: hermetic.com/bey/taz_cont.html

[31] Ord, J. (2004). *The Youth Work Curriculum and the 'Transforming Youth Work Agenda'.* Youth and Policy. Leicester: National Youth Agency. pp.53-85

[32] Ibid, pp.55-56.

[33] Ord, J. (2012). *Aristotle, Phronesis and Youth Work – measuring the process: a contradiction in terms.* In: 7th International Youth Work and Youth Studies Conference. University of Strathclyde. 28 Aug 2012. Available at: www.strath.ac.uk/media/faculties/hass/conferences/Jon_Ord_Presen tation.pdf

[34] Ibid, p.3.

[35] Wright, N.T. (2011). *Learning the language of life, new creation and Christian virtue.* Podcast. Available at: https://itunes.apple.com/us/itunes-u/n.t.-wright/id404625689

[36] Ibid, Ord, J. (2012). p.13.

[37] Government initiative. (2003). *Every Child Matters.* Available at: www.education.gov.uk/consultations/downloadableDocs/EveryChildM atters.pdf

[38] Cabinet Office and Department for Education. (2010). *Positive for Youth: a new approach to cross-government policy for young people aged 13 to 19*. Available at: www.gov.uk/government/publications/positive-for-youth-a-new-approach-to-cross-government-policy-for-young-people-aged-13-to-19

[39] PEDAGOGY OF THE OPPRESSED by Paulo Freire (Pelican Books 1972, Penguin Books, 1990, 1996). Copyright © Paulo Freire, 1970, 1993. Foreword by Richard Shaull. pp.13-14.

[40] Ministry of Education. (1960). *The Youth Service in England and Wales* ('The Albemarle Report'). London: Her Majesty's Stationery Office.

[41] Ibid, p.36.

[42] National Youth Bureau. (1991). *Towards a core curriculum – the next step. Report of the Second Ministerial Conference.* Leicester: NYB

[43] Parliament UK. (2011). House of Commons – Services for young people – Education. Available at: www.publications.parliament.uk/pa/cm201012/cmselect/cmeduc/744/74405.htm

[44] National Youth Agency (NYA). (2011). *What is youth work? Youth work in brief.* Available at: www.nya.org.uk/about-nya/what-is-youth-work

[45] Brierly, D. (2003). *Joined Up: An Introduction to Youth Work and Ministry.* Carlisle:Spring Harvest Publishing Division and Authentic Lifestyle. .pp 118-119

[46] Oxford Dictionaries online. (n.d.).*Definition of Power in English.* Available at: oxforddictionaries.com/definition/english/power?q=power

[47] Williams, R. (2011). *Changing the Landscape*. In: Changing the Landscape: making the mixed economy work conference. 6th May 2011, Oxford. Available at: www.freshexpressions.org.uk/changingthelandscape/2011/rowanwilliams

[48] Ibid, Ord, J. (2004) pp.55-56.

[49] Ibid, Ministry of Education (1960). Paragraph 187

[50] Goetchius, G. and Tash M. J. (1967). *Working with Unattached Youth: Problem, approach, method*, London: Routledge and Kegan Paul.

[51] Crimmens et al. (2004). *The role of street-based youth work linking socially excluded young people into education training and work.* Avaliable from www.jrf.org.uk/publications/role-street-based-youth-work-linking-socially-excluded-young-people-education-training.

[52] Fontaine, A. et al. (2008). *The International guide on the methodology of street work throughout the world*. Brussels: Dynamo International.

[53] Andrews, D. (1989) *Can you hear the heartbeat?* Philippians: OMF. p.31

[54] Arnold, J. et al. (1981). *The Management of Detached Work. How and Why*, Leicester: National Association of Youth Clubs.

[55] Federation for Detached Youth Work. (2012). *The Aims of Detached Youth Work*. Leicester: Federation for Detached Youth Work. Available at: www.detachedyouthwork.info/more_about_detached_youth_work.ht m#%27Aims%20of%20Detached%20Youth%20Work%27

[56] Goetchius, G. and Tash, M. J. (1967). *Working with Unattached Youth: Problem, approach, method*, London: Routledge and Kegan Paul. pp.93-95

[57] Sercombe, H. (2010). *Youth Work Ethics*. London: Sage Publications Ltd. p.26

[58] Vanhoozer, K. J. (2005). *The Drama of Doctrine: A Canonical Linguistic Approach to Christian Doctrine*. Louisville: Westminster John Know Press. p.313-314.

[59] Ibid, Goetshius, G. and Tash, M. J. (1967)

[60] Ibid, Pimlott, J. and Pimlott, N. (2008). p.76.

[61] Jeffs, T. and Smith, M.K. (2005). *Informal Education: Conversation, Democracy and Learning.* 3rd Ed. Nottingham: Educational Heretics Press.

[62] Smith, H. (2010). Engaging in conversation. In: Smith, M.K. and Jeffs, T. *Youth Work Practice*. Basingstoke: Palgrave MacMillan. p.32.

[63] Ibid.

[64] Blacker, H. (2010). Relationships, friendship and youth work. In: Smith, M.K. and Jeffs, T. *Youth Work Practice*. Basingstoke: Palgrave MacMillan. p.17.

[65] Ibid. p.16.

[66] Fontaine, A. et al. (2008). *The International guide on the methodology of street work throughout the world*. Brussels: Dynamo International.

[67] Putnam, R.D.(2001). *Bowling Alone: The Collapse and Revival of American Community*. New York: Touchstone. p.331.

[68] Clapp, R. (1996). *A Peculiar People: The Church as Culture in a Post-Christian Society*. Downers Grove: IVP. p.198.

[69] Ibid, Vanhoozer, K.J. (2005). p.3.

[70] Griffiths, S. (2008). *A Christlike Ministry.* Cambridge: YTC Press. pp.6-10.

[71] Pimlott, N. (2005). Spirituality With Young People. In: Pimlott. J., Pimlott, N. and Wiles, D. *Inspire Too! More fresh ideas for creative youth work.* Birmingham: Frontier Youth Trust. p.13.

[72] Ibid, p.11.

[73] Collins-Mayo, S. Mayo, B and Nash, S. (2010). *The Faith of Generation Y.* London: Church House Publishing. p.19

[74] Ibid, Brewin, K. (2011) pp.227-228

[75] Ibid. p.17

[76] Rankin, P. (2005). *Buried Spirituality: A Report on the Findings of the Fellowship in the Spirituality of Young People.* Salisbury: Sarum College Press.

[77] Ibid, Arbuckle, G.A. (1993). p.1

[78] Sanneh, L. (1989). *Translating the Message.* Maryknoll: Orbis. pp.29-30.

[79] Ibid, Donovan, V. (1996) p.122.

[80] Ibid, Vanhoozer, K.J. (2005). p.80

[81] Ibid. pp.116-120

[82] Ibid. p.129

[83] Ibid. p.57.

[84] Ibid. p.457.

[85] Boal, A. (2000). *Theatre of the Oppressed.* 3rd Ed. Translated by McBride, M.O.L. and Fryer, E. London: Pluto Press. p.xxi

[86] Ibid, Vanhoozer, K.J. (2005). p.335

[87] Ibid, Clap, R. (1996). p.189

[88] Ibid, Vanhoozer, K.J. (2005). p.435.

[89] Gay, D. (2011). *Remixing the Church: Towards an Emerging Ecclesiology.* London: SCM Press. p.72.

[90] McNeil et al. (2013). *Noticing the change – A Framework of outcomes for young people in practice.* Available at: youngfoundation.org/publications/noticing-the-change-a-framework-of-outcomes-for-young-people-in-practice/

Bibliography

Andrews, D. (1995). *Can you hear the heartbeat?* Philippians: OMF Literature inc.

Arbuckle, G. A. (2010). *Culture, Inculturation, and Theologians: A Postmodern Critique.* Collegeville: Liturgical Press.

Arbuckle, G.A. (1993). *Refounding the Church: Dissent for Leadership.* London: Geoffrey Chapman.

Arnold, J. et al. (1981). *The Management of Detached Work: How and Why.* Leicester: National Association of Youth Clubs.

Barker, C. (2000). *Cultural Studies: Theory and Practice.* London: SAGE Publications Ltd.

Bartholomew, C.G. Green, J.B. and Thiselton, A.C. (eds.). (2006). *Reading Luke: Interpretation, Reflection, Formation.* Cumbria: Paternoster Press.

Behler, C. (n.d.). *Habitus.* [online]. Available at: faculty.washington.edu/cbehler/glossary/habitus.html [Accessed on 31 May 2013].

Bevans, S. B. (2004). *Constants in Context: A Theology of Mission for Today.* (Schroeder, R. Ed). Maryknoll: Orbis Books.

Bevans, S.B. (2011). *Prophetic Dialogue.* (Schroeder, R. Ed). Maryknoll: Orbis Books.

Bey, H. (1991). *The Temporary Autonomous Zone, Ontological Anarchy, Poetic Terrorism.* [online]. Available at hermetic.com/bey/taz_cont.html [Accessed on 31 May 2013].

Biology online. (n.d.). *Symbiosis.* [online]. Available at www.biology-online.org/dictionary/Symbiosis [Accessed on 31 May 2013].

Blacker, H. (2010). Relationships, friendship and youth work. In: Smith, M.K. and Jeffs, T. *Youth Work Practice.* Basingstoke: Palgrave MaMillan.

Blower, S. (2012). *Towards A B-Boy Theology.* Diss. Bristol Centre for Youth Ministry.

Boal, A. (2000). *Theatre of the Oppressed.* 3rd Ed. Translated by McBride, M. O. L. and Fryer, E. London: Pluto Press.

Endnotes and Bibliography

Bourdieu, P. (1984). Distinction: A Social Critique of the Judgement of Taste. London: Routledge and Kegan Paul.

Bosch, D. J. (1991). *Transforming Mission: Paradigm Shifts in Theology of Mission*. New York: Orbis Books.

Brewin, K. (2011). *Other: Embracing Difference in a Fractured World*. London: Hodder & Stoughton.

Brierley, D. (2003). *Joined Up: An Introduction to Youth Work and Ministry*. Carlisle: Spring Harvest Publishing Division and Authentic Lifestyle.

Brueggemann, W. (2001). *The Prophetic Imagination.* 2nd Ed. Minneapolis: Fortress Press.

Bullock, S. and Pimlott, N. (2008). *Glimpses: youth work and spirituality*. Leicester: National Youth Agency

Cabinet Office and Department for Education. (2010). *Positive for Youth: a new approach to cross-government policy for young people aged 13 to 19*. [online]. Available at: www.gov.uk/government/publications/positive-for-youth-a-new-approach-to-cross-government-policy-for-young-people-aged-13-to-19. [Accessed on 31 May 2013].

Case, A. (n.d.). Hyper Culture, Cyborg Anthropology. [online]. Available at cyborganthropology.com/Hyperculture [Accessed on 31 May 2013].

Clapp, R. (1996). *A Peculiar People: The Church as Culture in a Post-Christian Society.* Downers Grove: Inter-Varsity Press.

Collins-Mayo, S. Mayo, B. and Nash, S. (2010). *The Faith of Generation Y*. London: Church House Publishing.

Crimmens et al. (2004). *The role of street-based youth work linking socially excluded young people into education training and work*. [online]. Available at: www.jrf.org.uk/publications/role-street-based-youth-work-linking-socially-excluded-young-people-education-training- [Accessed on 31 May 2013].

De Bono, E. (1995). *Parallel thinking: From Socratic to de Bono Thinking*. London: Penguin Books.

Demos. (2009). A scoping study concerning community empowerment issues relating to children and young people. [online]. Available at: ncvys.org.uk/UserFiles/Speaking %20Out/Research/Demos_CommunityEmpowermentReport_Oct09.p df [Accessed on 1 July 2013].

Donovan, V.J. (1996). *Christianity Rediscovered*. London: SCM Press.

Eckhart, M. (n.d.). *It is not necessary to understand this.* [online]. Available at: www.jeanbouchartdorval.com/jardin/meckhart52-imp.html [Accessed on 31 May 2013].

Federation for detached youth work. (2012). *Aims of detached youth work.* [online]. Available at www.detachedyouthwork.info/more_about_detached_youth_work.ht m [Accessed on 31 May 2013].

Fontaine, A. et al (2008). Dynamo International. *The International Guide on the methodology of street work throughout the world.* [online]. Available at www.touchproject.eu/content/international-guide-methodology-street-work-throughout-world [Accessed on 31 May 2013].

Freire, P. (1996). *Pedagogy of the Oppressed.* 2nd Ed. Translated by Bermman Ramos, M. London: Penguin Books.

Freire, P. (1998). *The Paulo Freire Reader.* (Freire, A.M.A. and Macedo, D. Eds.). London: Continuum International Publishing Group Ltd.

Gay, D. (2011). *Remixing the Church: Towards an Emerging Ecclesiology.* London: SCM Press.

Goetschius, G.W. and Tash, M.J. (1967). *Working with Unattached Youth; Problem, Approach, Method. The Report of an Enquiry Into the Ways and Means of Contacting and Working with Unattached Young People in an Inner London Borough.* London: Routledge and Kegan Paul.

Government Initiative. (2003). *Every Child Matters.* [online]. Available at www.education.gov.uk/consultations/downloadableDocs/EveryChildM atters.pdf [Accessed on 31 May 2013].

Graham, E. Walton, H. and Ward, F. (2005). *Theological Reflection: Methods.* London: SCM Press.

Endnotes and Bibliography

Grenz, S. J. and Franke, J.R. (2001). *Beyond Foundationalism: Shaping Theology in a Postmodern Context*. Louisville: Westminster John Knox Press.

Griffiths, S. (2008). *A Christlike Ministry*. Cambridge: YTC Press.

The Holy Bible: New International Version. (1986). Hodder & Stoughton Religious.

Infed.org. (n.d.). *Animateurs, animation, learning and change.* [online]. Available at www.infed.org/animate/b-animat.htm [Accessed on 31 May 2013].

Jeffs, T. and Smith, M.K. (2005). *Informal Education: Conversation, Democracy and Learning.* 3rd Ed. Nottingham: Educational Heretics Press.

Jeffs, T. and Smith, M.K. Eds. (2010). *Youth Work Practice.* 2nd Ed. Basingstoke: Palgrave Macmillan.

Kreider, A. (1986). *Journey Towards Holiness: A Way of Living for God's Nation*. Basingstoke: Marshall Pickering.

Lings, G. (2012). *Why Modality and Sodality thinking is vital to understand future church*. [online]. Available at: www.churcharmy.org.uk/ms/sc/sfc_talks.aspx [Accessed on 31 May 2013 at: sheffieldcentreresearch.wordpress.com/2012/03/modality-and-sodalitydynamics.doc].

McLaren, B. (2013). *The Story We Find Ourselves In: Further Adventures of a New Kind of Christian: Book 2.* San Francisco: Jossey-Bass.

McNeil et al. (2013). *Noticing the change – A framework of outcomes for young people in practice*. [online]. Available at: youngfoundation.org/publications/noticing-the-change-a-framework-of-outcomes-for-young-people-in-practice/ [Accessed on 31 May 2013].

Minear, P. S. (2007). *Images of the Church in the New Testament*. Cambridge: James Clarke & Co Ltd.

Moltmann, J. (1977). *Church in the Power of the Spirit*. Translated by Kohl, M. London: SCM Press.

Muers, R. (2005). *The Modern Theologians: An Introduction to Christian Theology Since 1918.* 3rd Ed. (Ford, D.F Ed). Chicester: Wiley-Blackwell.

Endnotes and Bibliography

National Youth Agency (NYA). (2011). *What is youth work? Youth work in brief.* [online]. Available at: www.nya.org.uk/about-nya/what-is-youth-work [Accessed on 13 May 2013].

National Youth Bureau. (1991). *Towards a core curriculum – the next step. Report of the Second Ministerial Conference.* Leicester:NYB.

Occupy together. (n.d.). *Occupy Together.* [online]. Available at www.occupytogether.org [Accessed on 31 May 2013].

Ord, J. (2012). *Aristotle, Phronesis & Youth Work – Measuring the Process: a contradiction in terms.* In: 7th International Youth Work and Youth Studies Conference. University of Strathclyde. 28 Aug 2012. [online]. Available at www.strath.ac.uk/media/faculties/hass/conferences/Jon_Ord_Presentation.pdf [Accessed on 31 May 2013].

Ord, J. (2004). The Youth Work Curriculum and the 'Transforming Youth Work Agenda'. *Youth and Policy No. 83 spring 2004.* Pp 43-59. Leicester: National Youth Agency

Oxford Dictionaries online. (n.d.).*Definition of Power in English.* [online]. Available at: oxforddictionaries.com/definition/english/power?q=power [Accessed on 31 May 2013].

Ozhegov, S. (2007). Explanatory Dictionary of Russian Language. Moskva: A. Temp.

Parliament UK. (2011). *House of Commons – Services for young people – Education.* [online]. Available at www.publications.parliament.uk/pa/cm201012/cmselect/cmeduc/744/74405.htm [Accessed on 31 May 2013].

Passmore, R. (2003). *Meet Them Where They're At*: Helping churches engage young people through detached youth work. Bletchley, Milton Keynes: Scripture Union.

Passmore, R. (2004). *Off the Beaten Track: A fresh approach to youth work and church based on Jesus' Travel.* Birmingham: Christian Education Publications.

Peterson, E.H. (2009). *The Message: The Bible in Contemporary Language.* Colorado Springs: NavPress.

Pimlott. J, Pimlott, N and Wiles, D. (2005). *Inspire Too! More fresh ideas for creative youth work.* Birmingham: Frontier Youth Trust.

Endnotes and Bibliography

Pimlott, N. (2007). *Y6 Grove Series, How to Develop a Youth Work Project learning from Noah.* Cambridge: Grove Books Limited.

Pimlott, J. and Pimlott, N. (2008). *Youth Work After Christendom.* Bletchley, Milton Keynes: Paternoster Press.

Putnam, R. (2001). *Bowling Alone: The Collapse and Revival of American Community.* London: Simon & Schuster Ltd.

Raapana, N. and Friedrich, N. (2005). *What is the Hegelian Dialectic?* [online]. Available at www.crossroad.to/articles2/05/dialectic.htm [Accessed on 31 May 2013].

Rankin, P. (2005). *Buried Spirituality: A Report on the Findings of the Fellowship in the Spirituality of Young People Based at Sarum College, Salisbury.* Salisbury: Sarum College Press.

Richardson, A. (1935). *Creeds in the Making: Short Introduction to the History of Christian Doctrine.* London: SCM Press.

Rollins, P. (2006). *How (Not) to Speak of God.* London: SPCK Publishing.

Rollins, P. (2011). *Insurrection: To Believe is Human; to Doubt, Divine.* London: Hodder & Stoughton.

Sacks, J. (2006). *To Heal a Fractured World: The Ethics of Responsibility.* London: Continuum International Publishing Group Ltd.

Sanneh, L. (1989). *Translating the Message.* Maryknoll: Orbis.

Schreiter, R. J. (1985). *Constructing Local Theologies.* London: SCM Press.

Sciabarra, C.M. (1995). *Ayn Rand: The Russian Radical.* 2nd Ed. Pennsylvania: Pennsylvania State University Press.

Sercombe, H. (2010). *Youth Work Ethics.* London: SAGE Publications Ltd.

Stiver, D. R. (1994). *The uneasy alliance between evangelicalism and postmodernism:a reply to Thiselton.* Paper presented at the southeastern Regional, March 25-26, 1994, Louisville, Kentucky.

University of Sussex. [n.d.]. *Bourdieu and 'Habitus'.* [online]. Available at www.powercube.net/other-forms-of-power/bourdieu-and-habitus/ [Accessed on 31 May 2013].

Endnotes and Bibliography

Vanhoozer, K.J. (2002). *First Theology: God, Scripture and Hermeneutics*. Nottingham: Inter-Varsity Press.

Vanhoozer, K.J. (2005). *The Drama of Doctrine: A Canonical Linguistic Approach to Christian Doctrine*. Louisville: Westminster John Knox Press.

Ward, P. (1996). *Growing up Evangelical*. London: SPCK publishing.

Williams, R. (2011). *Changing the Landscape*. In: Changing the Landscape making the mixed economy work conference. 6th May 2011. Oxford. [online]. Available at www.freshexpressions.org.uk/changingthelandscape/2011/rowanwilli ams [Accessed on 31 May 2013].

Wright, N.T. (2011). *Learning the language of life, new creation and Christian virtue.* [Podcast]. Available at itunes.apple.com/us/itunes-u/n.t.-wright/id404625689

Wright, N.T. (2010). *Surprised by hope: Rethinking Heaven, the Resurrection, and the Mission of the Church*. Grand Rapids: Zondervan.

Zaehner, R.C. (1997). *The Hutchinson encyclopaedia of living faiths*. Oxford: Helicon.